Perfect Money Saving

Smita Talati is a freelance financial journalist. She wrote the popular 'Money Makeover' column for the *Sunday Times* for five years and regularly contributes to the money pages of other newspapers and magazines, including the *Daily Telegraph, Evening Standard, Mail on Sunday* and *Cosmopolitan.* Her two previous books are *How to be a Financial Goddess* and *How to be a Property Goddess.*

Other titles in the *Perfect* series

Perfect Answers to Interview Questions – Max Eggert
Perfect Babies' Names – Rosalind Fergusson
Perfect Brain Training – Philip Carter
Perfect Best Man – George Davidson
Perfect Calorie Counting – Kate Santon
Perfect Confidence – Jan Ferguson
Perfect CV – Max Eggert
Perfect Detox – Gill Paul
Perfect Family Quiz – David Pickering
Perfect Interview – Max Eggert
Perfect Letters and Emails for All Occasions – George Davidson
Perfect Memory Training – Fiona McPherson
Perfect Numerical Test Results – Joanna Moutafi and Ian Newcombe
Perfect Numerical and Logical Test Results – Joanna and Marianna Moutafi
Perfect Party Games – Stephen Curtis
Perfect Personality Profiles – Helen Baron
Perfect Persuasion – Richard Storey
Perfect Positive Thinking – Lynn Williams
Perfect Presentations – Andrew Leigh and Michael Maynard
Perfect Psychometric Test Results – Joanna Moutafi and Ian Newcombe
Perfect Pub Quiz – David Pickering
Perfect Punctuation – Stephen Curtis
Perfect Readings for Weddings – Jonathan Law
Perfect Relaxation – Elaine van der Zeil
Perfect Slow Cooking – Elizabeth Brown
Perfect Speeches for All Occasions – Matt Shinn
Perfect Wedding Planning – Cherry Chappell
Perfect Wedding Speeches and Toasts – George Davidson
Perfect Weight Loss – Kate Santon
Perfect Written English – Chris West

Perfect
Money Saving

Smita Talati

BOOKS

Published by Random House Books 2011

10 9 8 7 6 5 4 3 2

First published in the United Kingdom in 2010 by
Random House Books
Random House, 20 Vauxhall Bridge Road,
London SW1V 2SA

www.rbooks.co.uk

Addresses for companies within The Random House Group Limited
can be found at: www.randomhouse.co.uk/offices.htm

The Random House Group Limited Reg. No. 954009

A CIP catalogue record for this book
is available from the British Library

ISBN 9781847945969

The Random House Group Limited supports The Forest Stewardship
Council (FSC), the leading international forest certification organisation.
All our titles that are printed on Greenpeace approved FSC certified paper
carry the FSC logo. Our paper procurement policy can be found at
www.rbooks.co.uk/environment

FSC   Mixed Sources

Typeset in Mini... by ...... Book .... Limited
Falkirk, Stirlings...

Printed in the U...

Contents

Introduction   xiii

Financial housekeeping
  Get yourself in order   1
    De-clutter your financial paperwork   1
    Divide and file bills and statements   2
    Collect discount coupons and vouchers   2
    Write down your financial dreams   3
    Write your financial CV   4
  Keep a monthly spending diary   6
    Collect all your receipts   7
    Look at where your money goes   7
    Highlight areas in which to make savings   8
    Pay your bills by direct debit   9
  Save and make money online   9
    Common types of fraud   9
    Price comparison sites   10
  Shop online   12
    Discount vouchers   13
    Cashback sites   13
    Collective buying sites   14
  Know your credit rating   15
    How credit rating works   16
    What credit reference agencies don't know   17

1 January

New Year's resolutions 18
  Cure your Christmas debts 19
  Make the most of the January sales 19
Food shopping 20
  Make your shopping VAT free 21
  Be supermarket savvy 22
  Food storage 23
  Foods in season this month 24
Cut household bills 24
Cheap treats 26
  Pamper yourself at home 26
  Eat out for half price 26
  Bring your own bottle 26
Turn clutter into cash 27
  Sort it out 27
  Re-use it: things to make and mend 28
Make money by selling on eBay 28
  Ten steps to becoming a successful eBay seller 29
Where to stash your saved cash 30

2 February

Food shopping 33
  Cut your supermarket bill in half 33
  Foods in season this month 34
  Be store-cupboard savvy 34
  Invest in a freezer 36
Tackle DIY jobs 39
Remedies and treatments 40
  Beauty treatments 40
  Home remedies 41
Valentine's Day 42
  Flowers 42
  Dining out 42
  Eating in 42

Pancake Day, Lent and Easter 43
    Lent savings 43
Earn by doing online surveys 44
    How to make money from online surveys 44
Get paid to shop 45

3 March

Food shopping 48
    Foods in season this month 48
    Perfect portions 48
Homemade cleaning products 49
Save on your spring wardrobe 51
    Charity shops and market stalls 52
    Factory outlets 53
    Discount chains 55
    Designer ranges at supermarkets 56
    Swap clothes 57
    Make your own clothes 57
Rewards cards 58

4 April

Food shopping 61
    Foods in season this month 61
Swap and barter your skills 62
Grow your own fruit and vegetables 62
    Getting started 63
    Compost your food waste 64
Let your house to a film or TV company 65
Tax credits 65
    Apply early 66
    Working Tax Credits 67
    Child Tax Credits 67
Capital gains tax 68
Inheritance tax 68

5 May
      Food shopping   71
    ·   Foods in season this month   71
      Take an early summer holiday   72
          Travel money   72
          Car hire   74
          Mobile phones   75
          Travel insurance   75
      Sell your house without an estate agent   76

6 June
      Food shopping   80
          Foods in season this month   80
          Make your own lunch   80
          Keep your kitchen free of flies   81
          Pick your own fruit and vegetables   81
      Make your own hampers   82
      Chic money-saving weddings   83
          Set a budget   83
          The service   83
          The reception   84
          The dress   84
          The honeymoon   86
      Student finances   86
          Apply for student finance   87
          Maintenance grants   88
          Paying back the loans   88

7 July
      Food shopping   90
          Bulk buying   90
          Foods in season this month   91
          Keeping cool   92
      Graduate accounts   93

Car boot sales 93
Cut the cost of holiday childcare 94
   Holiday clubs and activities 95
   Cheaper childcare 96
   Share the care 96
   Holiday projects 96
   Crafty cash 96
End-of-summer sales 97

8 August

Food shopping 99
   Foods in season this month 99
Cut the cost of summer motoring 99
   Save on MOT, repairs and maintenance 100
   Save on fuel 100
Cut the cost of a family day out 101
   Use Clubcard points and discount vouchers 101
   Travel for less 101
   Think ahead 102
   Organise a picnic 103
   Summer health 104
Take a staycation 104
   Beach trips 104
   Caravans and camper vans 105
   Camping 106
   Yurts and tipis 106
   Feather Down Farms 106
   The National Trust 107
Holiday for less 108
   House swapping 108
   Retreats 109
   Free bed 110
Restore last year's school uniforms 111

9 September

Food shopping   114
    Foods in season this month   114
    Stop frozen bread from getting soggy   114
Save on utility bills   115
    Gas and electricity   115
    Home phone and broadband   115
Money-makers   116
    Let out your spare room or garage   116
    Become a cosmetics rep   117
Student finances   119
    Student bank accounts   120

10 October

Food shopping   122
    Foods in season this month   122
    Go foraging   122
Make your home more energy efficient   123
    Install good insulation   123
    Switch off appliances   123
    Get a smart meter   124
    Turn down the thermostat   124
    Save energy in the kitchen   124
Autumn garden maintenance   125
    Scoop up garden leaves   125
    Protect gardening tools   125
Half-term treats   125

11 November

Food shopping   128
    Foods in season this month   128
    Faster baked potatoes   128
    Christmas preparations   129
Buy a repossessed property   129
Unclaimed assets   130

12 December

    Food shopping   132

        Share the cost and effort of Christmas cooking   133

        Stock up on drinks   134

    Decorating your home   136

        The Christmas tree   136

        Homemade decorations   136

    Inexpensive gifts   137

        Low-cost presents   137

        No-cost presents   138

Quick Reference Section

QR1 The 'big' financial stuff   141

    Current accounts   141

        Switching current accounts   142

        Different types of current account   142

        Overdrafts   142

    Mortgages   143

        Fixed rates   143

        Discounted and capped rates   143

        Tracker mortgages   144

        Offset/current account mortgages   144

        Paying off your mortgage early   145

    Savings   146

        Individual Savings Accounts   146

        National Savings and Investments   147

        Premium Bonds   147

        Save the change   148

        Sweep it away   148

    Investments   148

        Unit trusts   149

        Investment trusts   150

        Tracker funds   150

        Fund supermarkets   150

Pensions   151
   Tax relief   151
   Company pensions   152
   Personal pensions   153
   Stakeholder pensions   153
   Personal account pensions   153
Credit cards   154
   Make more than the minimum repayment   155
   Transfer to a 0% balance transfer card   155
   Don't shuffle your debts   156
Financial advice   156
   How to get good financial advice   157

QR2 Debt management   158
   The six-point plan for getting your finances
   back on track   158

QR3 Your money growth calculator   160

Introduction

Ever since the effects of the credit crunch began ricocheting around the world in the summer of 2008 nostalgic notions of thrifty living have been seeping steadily into the national consciousness. After several years in which we lived to excess – mortgaging our homes to the hilt, piling debts on to credit cards and loans and splashing out on fancy holidays, cars and designer labels – the banks finally pulled the plug on the supply of cheap, easy credit, and many of us found we had to readjust our lifestyles.

But with a 2.5 per cent hike in VAT on goods and services ushering in 2011 and higher taxes, National Insurance contributions, salary cuts and benefit freezes taking their toll, the romantic idea of cutting back to make ends meet is now a harsh reality for most us. And things are unlikely to improve in the short term. Economists warn that we are facing a decade of austerity and fiscal belt-tightening as rising prices combined with budget cuts mean we are getting less for our money than we did before. Saving on everything, from food and fuel to clothing, holidays and childcare, is now a priority for every household.

Supermarkets, retailers, travel firms and leisure outlets, financial service providers and website entrepreneurs have responded to this with a panoply of innovative incentives. Whether we're shopping for groceries or browsing on the high street, flicking through a newspaper or surfing the internet, we're besieged with eye-catching banners and lurid advertisements promising huge discounts and savings on everything from cans of baked beans to cases of wine, mobile phones, clothes and cosmetics, holidays and household furniture. Buy-one-get-one-free, two-for-one, loyalty cards and triple points, air miles, freebies, cashbacks and collective buying have become part of our daily lexicon.

After years of profligacy and foolhardy spending we are also redis-covering a deep satisfaction in the neglected arts of making and mending, recycling and revamping, swapping and sharing and growing and selling our own. Community spirit, thrifty living and shrewd shopping around have replaced the 'throw it out and buy a new one' mentality. Making the best out of what we have is the new Zeitgeist.

But despite the numerous television programmes showing us how to whip up gourmet meals on a budget and revamp our homes on a shoestring, the plethora of websites bulging with discount vouchers and price comparison tables, and the newspapers stuffed with pull-out coupons, offers of the week and freebies, many of us allow money-saving opportunities to slip by. Those big savings happen to be for things we don't want or need on that particular day or week, or we discover that, when push comes to shove, they'd actually end up *costing* us twice the amount of the saving. So we write them off as time-wasting gimmicks and end up paying the full price, while marvelling at friends who have somehow cracked the art of eating out at half price, getting paid to shop, bagging a free laptop or digital camcorder, refurbishing their kitchens and bathrooms for the cost of a cheap flight or paying for two family holidays by selling their junk on eBay.

Like many things in life, a little careful planning and preparation (and a dash of cunning) are required to navigate the minefield of money-saving and money-making opportunities and to make your cash work harder. Saving and making extra money is not so much about mastering hard economic theory but about making small but effective lifestyle changes and acquiring new habits.

For such changes to make a palpable difference to our pockets and future wealth, however, we have to incorporate them into our lifestyles gradually – and that is the purpose of this book. There are plenty of money-saving books and websites that show how you can cut your fuel bills by insulating your loft and turning down the thermostat by one degree, slash your grocery bill by planning weekly menus and reducing food waste and holiday for less by searching for cheap flights, hotels, rental cars and mobile phone tariffs. This book is not another money-saving manual that regurgitates all this good advice thematically (although it does cover all these subjects and more). Instead, it is a round-the-year, money-saving programme carefully designed to help implement these techniques into your lifestyle so that they become hard-wired into your subconscious.

Incorporating just a handful of thrifty tricks and a little financial savvy into your daily life month by month will allow you to pick up money-saving skills that will last a lifetime. By the end of the year you will have saved several thousands of pounds on food, clothing, household expenses and travel costs, and have laid firm foundations for accumulating even bigger savings and wealth the next year and the years after that. And these changes will have a beneficial knock-on effect on many other areas of your life: you'll find yourself eating more healthily, developing new skills and aptitudes, discovering new places, making new friends, and leading an altogether more satisfying and fulfilling life. Indeed, the great thing about acquiring the money-saving habit through a programme like this is that it has an enormous snowball effect on every area of your life.

Another reason for following a round-the-year money-saving programme is that, just like our food cupboards and wardrobes, our finances go through seasonal cycles. We all need more money for food, drink and presents around Christmas time, and most of us come up short and feel the pinch in January. It is easy to blow half your salary on the latest spring fashions in March, only to find them substantially reduced in price just a few months later. We can all make significant savings on summer holidays, fun days out, motoring costs and staycations, and most new students would benefit from a crash course in budgeting in September.

The *Perfect Money Saving* programme is organised into chapters for every month of the year. Each month you'll discover new ways of cutting your grocery bill, saving money on transport and leisure, updating your wardrobe and enjoying luxury treats for less, making significant savings on big-ticket purchases, or earning extra cash.

You'll learn how to cut VAT on your grocery shopping and turn your clutter into cash on eBay in January and how to get paid to shop in your lunch hour in mid-February. We'll ensure you claim all the tax credits that you're entitled to before the end of the tax year in April. You can save a fortune on childcare over the summer holidays by clubbing together with friends to share the cost, buying food in bulk, and downloading discount vouchers for fun days out at theme parks and zoos. World-class ballet and opera performances can be seen for free on outdoor screens around the country in July, and, by organising a house-swap, it is perfectly possible (and very fashionable) to enjoy a holiday abroad for the whole of August for little more than the cost of the flights. You can earn an extra £80 a week tax free by letting out your spare room to a student in September, and knock hundreds of pounds off your utility bills by turning down the central heating by just one degree in November. And we'll show you how to slash the cost of your Christmas bills by stocking up on cheap wines and gourmet foods on a quick trip to France, and by making homemade decorations, presents, stocking fillers and gift wraps.

This book is designed to save you money methodically over a calendar year, but you don't have to wait till next January to start. Indeed, you can pick up the book and start the programme any month of the year, and flick forwards or backwards according to your individual needs. Once you've stepped on to the money-saving treadmill you'll find it becomes quite addictive. You'll be constantly on the lookout for discounts, money-off vouchers and bargains as well as new ways and opportunities to sell, swap, re-use, recycle, customise, make and mend. Things that once seemed a bore, such as rustling up family meals from uninspiring leftovers or customising old clothes instead of going out and buying new ones, will become fun and second nature, just as they were in our grandparents' day.

Much of this book is about making small but significant savings on the minutiae of daily living. It is crammed with money-saving tips on everything from planning family meals to making money at car boot sales, but don't become disheartened if you do not embrace every idea. Making just one or two changes can have a big effect – in 1987 American

Airlines saved $40,000 by eliminating just one olive from every salad meal it served to first class passengers.

However, there's no point looking after the pennies if you throw away the pounds. To become a fully accomplished money saver you must also get the best deals on your bank account, mortgage, insurances, loans and credit cards; make maximum tax savings; and invest your hard-earned savings wisely. As well as saving money around the house and at the shops, the *Perfect Money Saving* programme will help you ensure you're on track with all the 'big' financial stuff. By the end of the year you'll have shaved several hundreds of pounds off your mortgage, home and car insurance, credit cards and loan bills, be reaping the rewards of compound interest on your savings, and have the confidence to invest in the stock market.

Nutritionists advise people who are embarking on a new diet to start by clearing out their fridge and kitchen cupboards. Similarly, the first step to becoming a perfect money saver is to give your finances a thorough spring clean. That is why, regardless of which month in the year you embark on the programme, we ask you to start by compiling your household's financial CV and monthly spending diary. This means collating receipts and jotting down where your money goes – at the supermarket, on train fares, or shopping on the internet. It also means taking stock of all your important financial products – mortgage, insurances, pensions and investments – and noting how much they cost each month, when they are up for renewal and whether their performance comes up to scratch.

When you have entered all your financial products into your financial CV, make a note in your diary to review all insurance policies, credit cards with introductory offers and your mortgage, at least *three months* before they expire. This way you won't get caught out with automatic renewal policies, which usually mean an increase in premiums or higher rates. It is surprising how much money you can save just by spending a few minutes shopping around and switching suppliers. For example, switching to a 1 per cent cheaper rate on a £100,000 mortgage could save you nearly £1,000 a year – enough for a nice holiday.

Banks, insurance companies and mortgage lenders thrive on

customer apathy. It's why all those tempting initial offers that lure you in with freebies, vouchers and air miles require you to sign up by direct debit. By all means, take up the initial offer, but don't get sucked in beyond the benefit period. A recent survey showed that remaining 'loyal' to banks and insurance companies instead of shopping around costs the average person over £800 a year. The perfect money saver shows great loyalty to family and friends, but not to financial services providers.

If you have debts or mortgage arrears turn to Quick Reference 2 for a debt management plan. By tackling creditors in the right way, making sure that you reclaim all unfair charges, and drawing up a manageable repayment plan, you can get your finances back on track. And, of course, by changing your spending habits through this programme you'll be less likely get into debt in the future.

As well as giving your finances a money-saving makeover, the *Perfect Money Saving* programme is also designed to get you on track to achieving your financial dreams. There's no point locking yourself into a five-year fixed-rate mortgage if you're hoping to move house in the next couple of years. And if you're planning to take a few years off work to have a baby, ditching the daily cappuccino and muffin, and putting the saved £50 a month into a high-interest savings account, will give you a nice little nest egg. The Centre for Economics and Business Research has calculated that new parents spend just over £9,000 on buggies, cots, nappies, clothes and toys in the first year of their child's life. The average cost of bringing up a toddler from the ages of one to four is almost £13,000 and the total cost of raising a child to the age of 21 is an eye-watering £200,000!

Saving money is not just about being sensible. It can be great fun too. You'll acquire new skills, develop your creative resources and make new friends. As you work through the programme month by month, record the savings you make on food, fuel, travel, entertainment, clothes and household bills and see how they accumulate on your money growth calculator. Watching your money grow is exhilarating and will give you the incentive to save and invest even more next month ... and the month after that. And you'll get a real buzz from seeing how it has a knock-on effect on other areas of your life.

So if you and your family are throwing away thousands of pounds on expensive mortgages and insurances, ready-made meals, gadgets, and clothes that only last a season or on wasted fuel and energy turn to this month's chapter and start the *Perfect Money Saving* programme today. You'll be richer, and feel healthier, happier and more energetic too.

To give you an idea of how the *Perfect Money Saving* programme could work for you, here's a breakdown of how a typical family of four could save over £6,000 in a year.

Change	£ saving
Switching to 1% cheaper mortgage	960
Summer holiday in May instead of August	1,120
Changing insurance providers	300
Switching utility providers	275
Saving gas & electricity	350
Avoiding food waste	640
Changing driving habits	150
Giving up daily cappuccino	828
Better home maintenance	250
Using discounts on family days out	400
Selling unwanted clutter	400
Making & mending	400
Total saving	**£6,018**

But this is just the tip of the iceberg – most of you will be able to save far more once you start, so if this has whetted your appetite, read on!

Financial housekeeping

Get yourself in order

Before you embark on your 12-month money-saving programme, it is important to:

- get your financial paperwork in order
- keep a monthly spending diary
- compile your financial CV and write down your financial goals
- know your credit rating
- familiarise yourself with online tools such as price comparison sites and money management software.

So no matter which month in the year you begin your *Perfect Money Saving* programme, work through this chapter first.

De-clutter your financial paperwork

Allowing unopened utility bills, credit card statements and insurance policies to pile up doesn't just clutter up your desk but also your mind. It makes daily life more stressful because there is always the quiet nag that those bills need paying, if only you could find the time to do so. Good financial housekeeping begins with devising an efficient system for organising all your financial paperwork and making sure that your bills are paid on time, by direct debit, so you never get caught out with late payment charges.

Divide and file bills and statements

If you receive bills and statements by post use one ring binder to file your monthly bank statements, with the most recent month at the front. Put all your household bills in another heavy-duty ring binder, separating them with subject dividers for the categories listed below. If you bank and pay your bills online organise your statements into folders on your computer for:

- Mortgage statements

- Credit card statements

- Gas and electricity

- Council tax

- Water rates

- Insurance policies

- Telephone, broadband and mobile phone.

If you work from home you should keep telephone and utility bills for seven years for tax purposes. Otherwise, throw out bills and statements that are over a year old. Just like sorting out a wardrobe or cupboard, giving your financial paperwork a thorough 'feng shui' will have a wonderful detoxifying effect on your life, and it will also make it easier to write your financial CV later on and focus your mind on financial aims for the short, medium and long term.

Collect discount coupons and vouchers

A multitude of money-saving opportunities comes in the form of coupons and vouchers in newspapers and magazines, direct mail leaflets, supermarket fliers, or e-vouchers printed off the internet. The nature of such discounts means that they are valid for only a limited period, and they often depend on you making certain purchases, so there is only a small window of opportunity to take advantage of them. So that you don't miss out cut out or print out every voucher or coupon you spot and think you may use and pop them into an envelope or folder. At the beginning of each week (when you are writing your shopping list) sift through them, pull out the ones that are valid for the coming week and attach them to a pinboard in your kitchen. At the end of the week discard any vouchers you haven't used so that you don't end up with a heap of expired, dog-eared coupons in the bottom of your bag.

Write down your financial dreams

What are you earning and saving money for? Do you want to move to a bigger house or new area in the next few years? Do you want to give up work to have a baby soon? Will your children be starting university in the next few years? Do you want to buy a new car or television or invest in a new kitchen, bathroom or loft conversion?

Good financial housekeeping is not about watching your pennies just for the sake of it. It is, more crucially, about making sure that your financial portfolio is in alignment with your financial dreams, so that you are on track to achieving all your financial goals for the short, medium and long term.

For example, if you want to take a career break to start a family in the next couple of years it could be worth ditching your gym subscription and putting the money into a savings account to build up a nest egg for when you stop work. The abolition of child trust funds and the Health in Pregnancy Grant, and the freezing of child benefit until 2013 mean that new mothers and their babies will be almost £1,000 worse off than in 2009. It would also be useful to start navigating the minefield of equipment, clothes and toys, and working out what you will definitely need to buy, what you can borrow from friends and family and what you can do without.

If you're planning to move house in the next year or so it's a good idea to draw up a plan of all those little DIY jobs that you have been putting off, so your home is in tip-top condition when you come to sell. Estate agent fees can be as much as 3 per cent of the eventual sale price, so it is also worth learning to sell your home yourself using one of the many online sites; on a £250,000 home this could save you over £7,000 in fees. And if you want to buy a new big-ticket item, such as a bed or television, or invest in a new kitchen or bathroom, it pays to plan ahead so that you can take advantage of seasonal offers and discounts – or maybe even scoop a freebie.

Before you begin to compile your family's financial CV write down your financial goals for the short, medium and long term, and next to each goal write the estimated cost of achieving it.

- Short-term goals (1–2 years)

- Medium-term goals (3–5 years)

- Long-term goals (5–10 years)

An example of each type of goal would be:

- Short-term goal – a family holiday for four to Disneyland (estimated cost £10,000)

- Medium-term goal – move from current three-bedroom house to a four-bedroom house (estimated cost £70,000)

- Long-term goal – help fund eldest child through university (estimated cost £15,000)

At first glance it might seem that acquiring such vast amounts of money is an impossible dream, but as you work through the *Perfect Money Saving* programme month by month you'll be surprised how the savings can add up, and how you can easily double the amount you save simply by making small changes.

Write your financial CV

The purpose of writing your household financial CV is to make sure that you are putting your money into the right products to achieve your financial dreams. In Quick Reference 1 we explain in more detail exactly how mortgages, savings, investments, pensions and insurance policies work and how you can choose the best products to achieve your short-, medium- and long-term financial goals.

In order to overhaul your financial portfolio, however, you need to know how it stacks up now, so write your financial CV by looking at the key areas of your finances and adding up your total monthly outgoings. It may take you some time to collate this information, but it will be quite illuminating to discover where your money goes each month and how your debts and assets stack up.

Your mortgage

How much do you owe on your home? How much do you pay each month? What interest rate are you paying? When does the rate expire? How many years are left on your mortgage? What is the estimated market value of your home? (You can get a rough idea of the probable value of your home by checking the sale price of similar properties in your postcode on www.houseprices.co.uk.)

Your savings

Make a note of the value of your savings and the rate of interest you are earning on your Premium Bonds, deposit accounts and cash ISAs.

Your investments

If you hold stocks and shares ISAs, save-as-you-earn schemes or individual shares make a note of how much each investment is worth.

Your pensions

If you are a member of a company pension scheme ask for a valuation of the pension fund from the human resources department. If you have a personal pension, how much is it worth?

Your insurance

How much do you pay for your home, car and life insurance each month? When do the policies come up for renewal? Can you find cheaper policies?

Your credit cards

If you are paying interest on your credit cards, how much are you paying each month? If you are making the minimum repayments, turn to the section on debt management in Quick Reference 2.

Online money management tools

If you bank and manage your credit cards, insurances, mortgage and utility bills online the most efficient way of keeping track of your finances is to register with a free, secure online money management tool. One of the best is www.moneydashboard.com. Simply enter all your account passwords into the system and the site will connect simultaneously to your financial and utility suppliers to provide an instant snapshot of where your finances stand. Your password information is securely fed through Yodlee, a financial aggregator system renowned for its security used by the Bank of America and the US gold reserve at Fort Knox.

Another useful feature of this site is that it can 'tag' your expenditure by categories so you can see exactly how much you are spending each month on food, clothing, fuel, utilities or entertainment. Money Dashboard will also work out how much money you have left each month to save.

Keep a monthly spending diary

Your financial CV addresses the big financial stuff – how much you owe on your home, how much your retirement pot is worth, whether you have sufficient savings and investments for short-, medium- and long-term financial dreams and how much all this costs you each month. However, the bulk of the savings you will make by working through the *Perfect Money Saving* programme will be through your day-to-day living expenses.

Indeed, the real key to accumulating wealth is to plough the savings you make on the minutiae of daily life into your bigger savings and investments. For example, if you manage to save an extra £100 a month on your grocery shopping, household bills and leisure expenses and use this to make overpayments on a £100,000 mortgage you would save yourself £27,000 over 25 years and pay off your entire mortgage six years early. That would be enough to help fund one child through university and take the family on a once-in-a-lifetime holiday. Over the next month, keep a spending diary and see how much extra cash you can put to better use for your financial future.

Collect all your receipts

Get into the habit of collecting all the receipts and bills for every-thing you buy, and record everything you spend money on in your spending diary. It's important to note down all the little things – the magazine you buy at the station, the can of drink you get from the vending machine at the gym and the odd bottle of wine you run out to buy from the off-licence – as well as the weekly grocery shop, filling up at the petrol station and buying a new pair of shoes. You may be surprised to discover just how much you spend on these little impulse purchases.

Look at where your money goes

At the end of the month pull out all the receipts and bills, look through your spending diary and make a note of where your money goes each month in a table like the one below. You can add extra categories if you need to.

	£ spent
Food & drink	
Household goods & sundries	
Gas & electricity	
Water	
Telephone	
Council tax	
TV license	
Petrol	
Travel	
Clothes & shoes	
Eating out & entertainment	
Days out	
Books, CDs & DVDs	
Newspapers & magazines	
Hairdressing & beauty treatments	

Highlight areas in which to make savings

As you work through this book you'll pick up numerous new ways of substantially cutting your spending each month. You will also discover ways of making extra cash. However, it is quite likely that you will identify areas in which you've been unnecessarily profligate just by looking at your diary. For example, did you fill your supermarket trolley with fresh meat and vegetables and then leave them to rot in the fridge because you decided to eat out three times last week? Did your jaw drop when you opened your last gas bill and realised that you had left the heating on all night? Are you paying subscriptions for gyms or clubs you hardly use? Do you buy a daily newspaper when you could read the same articles for free online? Over the next 12 months you will be replacing these expensive habits with better, cheaper ones, but note down any ways in which you could make savings right away.

Pay your bills by direct debit

Good financial housekeeping means knowing exactly where your money goes each month and making sure that you're on top of all bills. Paying your bills by direct debit could potentially save you hundreds of pounds because you'll avoid accumulating late-payment fees and most utility suppliers offer discounts to customers who set up regular direct debits. You should also pay your council tax by direct debit. If you miss more than two monthly payments, your local authority may instruct bailiffs to recover the debt and threaten you with court action.

Save and make money online

As you will see from the sections that follow, by far the greatest savings on everything from grocery shopping to financial products, utility supplies, holidays and travel, books, electrical goods and leisure pursuits can be found online. There are also numerous legitimate and often quite lucrative ways of earning extra cash online, including completing online surveys, entering competitions, shopping on cashback sites and selling your goods.

There are, however, also thousands of online scams, so it is important to learn to differentiate between genuine sites and bogus ones. Research by the life assistance company CPP found that a quarter of all internet users have been victims of financial fraud at some point and that cybercrime afflicts one user every seven seconds.

Common types of fraud

- *Exploiting current disasters.* In May 2010 many bogus sites exploiting the volcanic ash from Iceland appeared, asking travellers for passport details to get refunds for airline tickets.

- *Fake recruitment agencies.* Never give your bank or passport details when you sign up with online recruitment agencies.

- *Bogus competitions and prize websites.* This is where you need to be really discerning, because although there are numerous legitimate competition websites and opportunities to win prizes and make money online through surveys, focus groups and mystery shopping, there are also numerous scams. If the offer sounds too good to be true it most likely is.

For more information on shopping and banking safely online, visit www.getsafeonline.org. Get Safe Online is a joint initiative between the government, businesses, the public sector and law enforcement agencies, explaining what features to look for on online financial and shopping sites and also how to report any suspicious-looking sites.

Price comparison sites

One of the quickest perceived ways of finding the best deal on everything from car insurance to utility suppliers and camcorders is to use a price comparison website. However, with over a hundred such sites to choose from in this bitterly competitive billion-pound industry, you really need a comparison site to compare the comparison sites. No single site has all the best prices, so you will need to visit two or three to find that elusive best deal, and, according to research from the University of East Anglia's Centre for Competitive Policy, although one-fifth of customers using a price comparison site will get the best deal, another fifth will actually end up paying more.

Price comparison sites make money through commercial arrangements with the companies they list. The sites are paid a commission when a customer either purchases a product or clicks through from the site to a company's own website. Needless to say, this greatly skews the deals on offer because consumers have no way of knowing how much commission a site receives from any single company. The online industry is a fast-moving, fast-changing one, so commissions and incentives fluctuate from week to week, and prices and quotes vary significantly. Indeed, it is not uncommon to find as much as a

50 per cent price difference between the 'best buy' product on two different sites.

It is also worth remembering that some companies, such as Direct Line and Aviva, do not list themselves on price comparison sites, so it is worth contacting them direct to see if they can beat whatever deals the comparison sites throw up. Follow the guide below to make sure you get the best deal from these sites.

- *Use more than one site.* No one site has all the best deals so use at least two, ideally three, different sites to compare quotes.

- *Fill in the form carefully.* Comparison sites provide the majority of new business for most insurance companies. In a bid to make their policies as cheap as possible, many insurance application forms automatically default to a large excess or limited cover. It is easy to click through and accept these options in a bid to finish the application as quickly as possible and buy the cheapest policy that comes up, only to discover that you are underinsured when you make a claim. It is a good idea to note down what levels of cover you require *before* you start to fill out the form. Double-check that the policy meets your requirements before you purchase.

- *Do not automatically renew your policy at the end of the year.* Insurance is a competitive and fast-changing industry, and your existing provider may not offer the best deal next year, so shop around again when your policy comes up for renewal.

Top price comparison sites

Financial services and utilities

- www.moneysupermarket.com – has thousands of deals on insurance, loans, credit cards, mobile phone tariffs and mortgages.

- www.confused.com – compares quotes on insurances, credit cards, loans and energy bills.

- www.uswitch.com – was one of the first comparison sites to appear, and allows you to compare energy, broadband, credit card, insurance, home and mobile phone quotes.

- www.gocompare.com – gives motoring quotes from over 120 different insurers; it also compares travel insurance, energy tariffs, loans and home insurance.

Shopping and groceries

- www.mysupermarket.co.uk

- www.ciao.co.uk

- www.kelkoo.co.uk

- www.pricerunner.co.uk

Shop online

You can buy just about anything you want at the click of a mouse and often for much less than you would in a store, but before you complete an online order always check the following:

- returns policy

- delivery charges

- when you will get the goods.

In addition, familiarise yourself with discount voucher sites, cashback shopping sites and collective buying sites. As you will soon discover, they can save you thousands of pounds a year.

Discount vouchers

Before you plan a day out, book a meal or theatre trip or make a purchase check what discount vouchers are available. The online discount voucher industry has become big business, and there are numerous discount shopping websites teeming with offers.

Two types of discount voucher are available online. As the term suggests, printable vouchers are coupons you print off from your computer and hand in to the cashier; they are typically two-for-one offers at restaurants, cinemas or theme parks. The other type of voucher is a voucher code, which can be redeemed only when you buy online. The voucher will include a link to the retailer and a code that you need to type in when you go to the checkout to receive your discount. Discount vouchers can save you hundreds of pounds over a year, so it is worth becoming familiar with a couple of the sites shown here. Remember to check the voucher's expiry date and also delivery charges before finalising your purchase.

> ## Top discount voucher sites
>
> - www.myvouchercodes.co.uk
> - www.savoo.co.uk
> - www.everydaysale.co.uk
> - www.vouchercodes.co.uk
> - www.fixtureferrets.co.uk

Cashback sites

Cashback sites work rather like supermarket reward cards; if you want to buy a washing machine from Currys, a crew-neck sweater and pair of deck shoes from Marks & Spencer, or a home insurance policy from Tesco, buy them through a cashback website rather than the retailer's site itself and you will get paid for your purchases.

In a bid to increase shopping traffic, retailers and financial services companies pay cashback sites commission each time a customer buys something through them, and to encourage you to shop through them again, the cashback site shares some of this commission with you. The most generous cashbacks tend to be paid by financial services providers – for example, Aviva (which does not list itself on price comparison sites) pays £70 to customers purchasing an insurance policy through a typical cashback site.

To take advantage of cashback shopping you will need to set up a free account with a site. Each time you want to buy something online, log on to the site, do your shopping from there and see your rewards accumulate. Some sites give you cashback in the form of payments through BACs or PayPal, whereas others pay in gift vouchers. With some sites you have to achieve a certain threshold before they pay you.

To double your savings use a cashback credit card to pay for your items when you shop through a cashback site. Cashback credit cards work in a similar way to cashback shopping sites. – that is, each time you make a purchase on your card the credit card provider pays a tiny percentage in cashback. With the most generous introductory offers this can be up to 5 per cent of the purchase amount. As long as you pay off your credit card each month this really is money for free, and by using it to shop on cashback sites you'll enjoy double savings.

Top cashback sites

- www.topcashback.co.uk
- www.quidco.com
- www.cashbackkings.com

Collective buying sites

Buying in bulk to gain a discount is nothing new, so it was only a matter of time before canny website entrepreneurs caught on to the idea of turning it into an online business.

Collective buying sites offer big discounts on things like theatre tickets, restaurant meals, experience days such as motor sports and paintballing, and spa breaks and beauty treatments. They do this by providing their suppliers with a guaranteed number of bookings. Therefore, an offer for a half-price ticket to a West End show or 70 per cent off a spa break will come to fruition only if a certain number of people sign up for it within a limited time. This is known the 'tipping point', and your payment will be collected only when the tipping point has been achieved, so you have nothing to lose if the deal does not come off. Some offers expire within 24 hours; others may run for up to a week. One of the longest established collective buying sites is www.wahanda.com, which offers fantastic discounts on spa breaks and beauty treatments. Collective buying sites are a great place for picking up cheap gifts for Mother's Day, birthdays and Christmas.

Top collective buying sites

- www.groupola.com

- www.mycitydeal.co.uk

- www.wowcher.co.uk

- www.wahanda.com

- www.likebees.com

Know your credit rating

Two credit reference agencies, Experian and Equifax, hold credit files on the vast majority of citizens in Britain. Before they offer you a credit card, loan, mortgage or overdraft financial institutions will credit score you, using the information provided by one of these agencies, to assess how likely you are to pay the money back. In the wake of the credit crunch lenders have tightened their criteria for assessing potential customers, and most now 'cherry pick' the best applicants for the most attractive deals. Just one missed or late payment on a credit card, loan or mobile phone bill could knock you out of the running for the most attractive financial deals, so, as you will see below, it is also important to make sure that you are on the electoral roll and to check that your partner or spouse (or anyone with whom you hold any joint accounts) has an equally clean credit history.

How credit rating works

Nobody has a universal credit score, and, contrary to popular opinion, there is no such thing as a 'credit blacklist'. Each lender will assess you against its own lending criteria, and even if you are turned down for a loan, credit card or mortgage by one provider you may well be accepted by another. Lenders also credit score applicants to decide which rates and products they will offer you. You are far more likely to be offered a favourable mortgage or loan rate if you score highly in your credit assessment.

Credit reference agencies hold the following information about you:

- Whether you are on the electoral roll and which other people live with you.

- Court records, including any county court judgements and bank-ruptcies.

- Search, address and linked data – that is, records of lenders that have searched your file, your previous addresses and information about anyone with whom you have a financial association, such as your partner, spouse or co-applicant on a mortgage.

- Fraud data – if you have committed financial fraud, or if someone has stolen your identity and committed fraud, this will be recorded on your credit file.

- Account data for all your accounts – bank accounts, loans, mortgages and credit cards, and also mobile phone accounts. Prospective lenders will be able to see how much you owe on all your debts, how much you repay each month – for example, if you clear your balance in full or just make the minimum payment each month – and whether you have defaulted on any accounts. They will also be able to see if you regularly shuffle your debts between credit cards offering 0 per cent on balance transfers.

What credit reference agencies don't know

Credit references agencies *do not* hold information on parking and driving fines, your salary or income, savings accounts, criminal records, medical records or student loans, nor do they have account details of family relations or other people living at your address (unless you share a joint account with them).

How to check your credit file – and get paid for it

You can check your credit file using Experian's Credit Expert or Equifax's Credit Gold Watch. Both offer a subscription service with a free 30-day trial, so you can check your file for free by signing up for the trial period and then cancelling your subscription straight away. You can also get paid to check your file by signing up for your free trial through a cashback website. In the summer of 2010 www.topcashback.co.uk was offering £5 for signing up to an free trial on Equifax.

Now turn to the appropriate chapter for this month to find out how to save money at the supermarket, on household bills, travel, clothes, and family days out. You'll change the way you shop and live forever, and start enjoying a wealthier, happier, healthier, leaner and greener life.

1 January

January is the traditional month for making resolutions. Most of us start the New Year with all guns blazing, determined to make *this* the year in which we change job, run the marathon, renovate the kitchen or become fluent in Spanish. But all too often we abandon these high-minded aspirations once the euphoria of the New Year wears off and the drudgery and bleakness of midwinter set in.

Dr Cliff Arnal, a psychologist at Cardiff University, is said to have coined the expression 'blue Monday', for the third Monday in January and calculated it to be the most depressing day of the entire year. Apparently, the combination of failed New Year's resolutions, Christmas debts, dark nights, low motivation and miserable weather takes its toll on us around then. It is precisely at times like this that we feel like splashing out on a skiing holiday, a spa weekend, a new coat or a pair of shoes just to cheer ourselves up. But as a 2.5 per cent hike in VAT ushers in 2011, going for a quick retail pick-me-up will burn an even bigger hole in your pocket than ever before.

New Year's resolutions

This year beat the January blues by blitzing your debts, making substantial savings on your supermarket shopping and turning unwanted Christmas presents and clutter around the house into hard cash or craft projects. By the end of the month, not only will you be several pounds richer, you'll also feel more refreshed and have discovered renewed energy and vitality to get those New Year's resolutions back on track.

Cure your Christmas debts

How bad is your Christmas hangover? Is your head still aching from the one before last? A survey by Money Expert found that in January 2009 one in eight credit card customers were still paying off their debts from Christmas 2007, and some were still paying off Christmas debts from a decade ago. Allowing debts to roll up like this is dangerous – you're slipping into a downward spiral, and the deeper you slide, the longer and more painful it is to climb back up. Like in a game of snakes and ladders, it's all too easy to slither down into the red, but it's a long, hard graft to climb back into the black again. So, if you have accumulated a mountain of debts turn to the section on debt management at the end of this book and tackle them head on, now.

Make the most of the January sales

It is all too easy to get caught up in the frenzy of the January sales and come home laden with clothes and gadgets you don't really want or need. Research by Bright Grey, life insurance specialists, found that in 2010 UK shoppers bought £2 billion worth of goods in the January sales that they later deemed to have been a waste of money. Nearly two-thirds of women bought clothes in the sales that they never wore, and one in ten women admitted to buying clothes in a smaller size than they actually wore in the hope of losing weight later in the year. Just over a third of male shoppers splurged out on new TVs, games consoles and stereos.

But the January sales are not necessarily the best time in the year to bag a bargain. Discount website www.savoo.co.uk tracked retailers' offers throughout the year and found that, whereas baby clothes were discounted by up to 40 per cent in the January sales, the best time to buy gadgets and electrical goods is actually March, April and July, when retailers slash their prices by up to 20 per cent. It also found that clothes and accessories are reduced by a much greater margin in the July sales than in the January sales. This may not be much consolation if you want a pair of boots or a cashmere sweater, but it is worth bearing in mind if you are buying all-season mix and match items.

Is the sale price a genuine bargain?

For an item to be put 'on sale' it must have been on sale previously at the full price in a number of stores. That doesn't necessarily mean that the 'sale price' is a good deal, however, particularly in January 2011, when an extra 2.5 per cent VAT is levied on goods. All retailers increase their prices for the big Christmas spend in December, so any 'reduction' in January may simply reflect the item's usual price. To make sure you're really striking a bargain in the January sales, follow this plan:

1. Decide exactly what items you want. Research by Bright Grey found that 54 per cent of consumers surveyed shopped spontaneously in the January sales.

2. Set a budget for your item(s) and stick to it.

3. Compare prices on the internet and in the shops. Ideally you should have started doing this in December so that you know whether the 'sale' price is a genuine bargain. If it isn't, chances are that the item(s) will be available at the same price (or cheaper) later in the year.

4. If the 'sale' price isn't a genuine bargain but you really want to buy it now, try haggling to get the price down. The fact that the item is 'on sale' means the shop is keen to get rid of it, so impress on the assistant that you require an incentive to buy it *today* or you'll simply walk away.

Food shopping

The average British family throws away a shocking £640 worth of food a year, so you won't be surprised to learn that a key component of the *Perfect Money Saving* programme is to change the way you shop, cook and store food. This means buying food when it is in season, planning menus for the week ahead, making a shopping list before you head for the supermarket, and storing and using what you buy correctly.

Make your shopping VAT free

In January 2011 VAT rises from 17.5 to 20 per cent, and the price comparison website www.mysupermarket.co.uk has estimated that this will add an extra £33 to the average annual supermarket bill. However, by changing the contents of your shopping basket, you can avoid paying any VAT on a substantial portion of your weekly shop.

VAT law is complicated and subject to all sorts of anomalies, but the basic rule is that essential foods are not subject to VAT, but 'luxury' goods are. The difficulty lies in working out exactly what the VAT man determines to be 'essential' and 'luxury'. Ready-made meals and hot takeaway foods, such as roast chickens, sausages and curries, are deemed to be 'luxury' items and so subject to VAT, but freshly baked foods, such as bread, are not. Wheat-based snacks, such as tortilla chips, fall into the 'essentials' category and are not subject to VAT, but potato crisps are a luxury and cost an extra 20 per cent. The biggest price difference is with dried fruits and nuts. If you purchase these items from the baking aisle, they fall into the zero-VAT category, but if you buy nuts and raisins packaged as 'snack foods' they become luxury items and you will pay VAT. Confused? Well, it keeps VAT officers in work.

Luxury foods (on which you pay 20% VAT)

Takeaway hot foods, cereal bars, partly or wholly covered chocolate shortbread, potato crisps, raisins packaged for snacks, ready-made popcorn, ice cream and ice lollies, crystallised ginger and chocolate-coated biscuits.

'Essential' items (on which you pay no VAT)

Freshly baked foods (such as bread), flapjacks, ginger in syrup, raisins packaged as a baking ingredient, microwave popcorn, vegetable crisps and wheat-based crisps (such as tortillas), milk and flavoured milks and chocolate-chip biscuits.

Be supermarket savvy

Supermarket aisles and shelves are carefully designed to entice you to spend as much money as possible. Marketing experts use every trick in the book to encourage you to slow down, make impulse purchases, bulk buy or try expensive new foods. Here are just a few of the tricks they use to entice you to buy things you don't want or need.

- Fresh flowers, household plants, gleaming displays of exotic fresh fruits and glossy magazines usually greet you when you enter the supermarket. The aim is to stall your progress into the store and tempt you to buy before you even get to the grocery shelves. If these items are not on your list walk straight past. You can always go back and pick up your weekly TV guide later.

- Pre-packed and loose vegetables are often placed side by side. It is tempting to quietly grab a pre-packed broccoli or bag of peppers, especially when the aisle is cluttered with other shoppers and trolleys, but it is cheaper to buy vegetables loose. This way you only buy the amount you need and can select the freshest produce.

- Ready-to-eat and ripened peaches, kiwi fruits, plums, tomatoes and avocados can be twice as expensive as slightly under-ripe produce. Ripen avocados at home by placing them in a brown paper bag with a banana.

- Ready-made meals, pasta sauces and frozen foods are carefully positioned to 'block' your way to essential food items, such as milk and tinned foods, to tempt you to top up your trolley before you get to the checkout. If ready-made chicken tikka masala and gourmet frozen cheesecakes are not on your list, walk straight past them.

- Supermarket own brands and basic ingredients are usually placed at the top, bottom or end of shelves or aisles, so your eye is automatically drawn to more expensive brands and gourmet delights. Train yourself to look specifically for own-brand cornflakes, basic salad dressings and plain biscuits.

- Colourful displays at the end of aisles sporting large, eye-catching discount banners often consist of excess stock selling at regular prices.

Of course, one of the most irritating things about supermarkets is that as soon as you've mastered the layout of your regular store the displays are re-arranged again. This is why it is vital to make a list before you head for the supermarket (and keep to it), dodge the clever layouts, and train your eye to look up, down and around for the items you want.

Avoid impulse purchases

Research shows that the average supermarket shopper makes at least one impulse purchase from every aisle. If your regular supermarket has ten aisles and you make just one impulse purchase costing £1 every week, you are throwing away at least £520 a year on unwanted food.

Compare the unit price of items

When you are looking at prices, make a point of comparing the unit price of similar goods rather than the actual price – that is, check the 'price per 100ml' or 'price per kilo'. This is particularly important when pack sizes vary or when you become dazzled choosing between an own-brand product and a large price reduction on a branded product – a three-for-two offer on a branded olive oil or toothpaste, may, for example, work out cheaper than the supermarket's own brand. You will quickly discover that larger sizes are not always the cheapest and that the cheapest items are usually tucked away at the top and bottom of shelves and aisles. By comparing the unit price of items you can save up to 50 per cent on your shopping bill.

Food storage

Do you dump your fruit and vegetables in the fridge without a second's thought as soon as you get home, only to find the lettuce has gone limp, or the broccoli mouldy, two days later? This is a money-wasting habit. Learn to store foods correctly, and you will prolong their life considerably. For example, wrapping cheese in a napkin soaked in salty water will stop it going mouldy.

Line the vegetable crisper drawer of your fridge

Start by lining the crisper drawer of your fridge with dry sponges. This will soak up the moisture that collects at the bottom of the drawer and which makes fresh vegetables rot. When you notice the sponges are wet, wring them out and leave them out to dry, before replacing them. Every now and then, soak them in warm water with a splash of bleach to stop them going mouldy.

Foods in season this month

Eating locally produced foods in season is not just cheaper, but more nutritious, appetising and interesting. For each month we include a list of foods that are in season and show how to pick some of the freshest produce and store it correctly. Foods to buy this month include carrots, leeks, scallops, shallots, squash and turnips.

Choosing and storing carrots: Look for carrots that are firm, not flabby, and that still have the green tops attached to them. Avoid carrots that show signs of sprouting or splitting. Top and tail unwashed carrots and parsnips and store them in an airtight container and they'll last for weeks and weeks.

Choosing and storing leeks: Buy small or medium-sized leeks, as larger ones tend to be tough and woody. Look for fresh, green tops and unblemished roots. Loosely wrap leeks in plastic and store them in the fridge where they should stay fresh for up to a week.

Choosing squash: Pick squash that still have their stems attached and that feel heavier than same-sized counterparts.

Choosing turnips: Look for turnips that look firm, are heavy for their size and have smooth, undamaged surfaces.

Cut household bills

The era of cheap energy is over, but you don't need to live in the dark, shiver in your thermals or discard your television and laptop to reduce your utility bills. Simply by making some small changes around the home you will be able to trim your bills quite substantially and also help reduce climate change. Our homes are responsible for over a quarter of carbon dioxide emissions that harm the environment, so using less energy will benefit everyone in the long term. Start the New Year by using your washing machine more efficiently, preventing dripping taps and replacing expensive, energy-guzzling light bulbs.

Cut washing costs

Get into the habit of waiting until you have a full load before you use the washing machine. Wash your clothes at 40°C rather than 60°C and you'll save at least a third on electricity.

Don't be a drip

Replace washers on dripping taps and make sure that everyone in the house gets into the habit of turning off the taps fully in the kitchen and bathroom. Dripping taps can add over £18 a year to your water bill.

Light bulb moment

Replace any incandescent light bulbs with energy-efficient ones and you'll save £60 in electricity over the bulb's lifetime – that's a saving of £600 a year.

Use an old umbrella as an indoor drying rack

Save on tumble-drying costs by using an old umbrella as a drying rack. Strip off the fabric and suspend the frame of the umbrella upside down from the shower rail in the bathroom. Attach wet clothes to the rack with clothes pegs. They will dry more quickly and more evenly than on the radiator, and any drips will fall into the bath. Simply fold away the umbrella when you've finished.

Cheap treats

January evenings are long, cold and dark, so indulge in some winter warmth with these cheap treats.

Pamper yourself at home

Foot warmer
Instead of racking up your gas bill by switching on the fire, fill a large plastic bottle with hot (not boiling) water, settle down on the sofa and roll it back and forth under your feet.

Luxury bath
Grind 25g of oatmeal in a blender, put it in a cheesecloth bag and add a few drops of scented oil. Suspend the bag under running water as you fill the bath, and use the cheesecloth bag as a scrub cloth to exfoliate your skin.

Eat out for half price

Get a wall-hanger in which to save up coupons and discount vouchers for restaurants, cinemas, theatres and family days out. Get into the habit of eating out midweek rather than at weekends, and book the restaurant online at www.toptable.com or www.5pm.co.uk to save up to 50 per cent off your bill at restaurants around the country.

Bring your own bottle

Most restaurants routinely put a 100 per cent mark-up on wine, but the days of paying £25 for a bottle of wine that retails for little more than £3 are over. Bring your own (BYO) restaurants are a way of life in Australia and some parts of the USA, and they are growing in popularity over here too. Look at www.wine-pages.com/food/byoblist for a list of BYO restaurants around the country.

Turn clutter into cash

Our homes and offices are swamped with far too much clutter and packaging, even though the 'throw it away and go out a buy a new one' mentality is bad for the environment, harmful to our pockets, and totally out of sync with the new age of austerity. There are dozens of opportunities to sell, swap and recycle everything from clothes and shoes, to homemade crafts and foods, gadgets and household goods, and such schemes can prove highly lucrative. Indeed, it is perfectly possible to finance an entire year's mortgage payments by scouting around for new household goods on recycling sites, making homemade cards and presents, and selling unwanted goods on eBay and at car boot sales.

Sort it out

Set aside a Sunday afternoon in which to go through all your cupboards and wardrobes for clothes, books, gadgets, household items and bric-a-brac. Then sort them into two piles: one of items you still use, another of items you haven't used in the last three months and would ordinarily throw out. You could be altruistic and donate the unwanted items to a local charity shop, or you could turn them into hard cash by selling them on eBay or at a car boot sale. The same goes for all those unwanted Christmas presents that can't be returned to the shops.

Track down lost manuals

Before you throw away an old camera or computer just because you've lost the instruction manual, check if you can track it down on www.instruction-manuals.co.uk.

Re-use it: things to make and mend

Designate a 'presents' cupboard in which you can store leftover wrapping paper, envelopes, present trimmings, jam jars, bottles, plastic tubs, tubes, boxes, bubble wrap, paper clips, rubber bands, pegs and pins. Also get into the habit of collecting free cosmetic samples, notepads and pens, souvenir bags and other goodies sent from marketing companies or picked up from hotel rooms, flights and promotions tables in stores. Over the year use these to make homemade gifts, hampers and stocking fillers, or to package up items to sell at car boot sales or on eBay.

Store it away for next year

Store away all your unused Christmas cards, decorations, wrapping paper and non-perishable foods for next year. Put them in a box and label it clearly so that you can find it in December.

Make money by selling on eBay

eBay was founded in 1995 as an online 'flea market', and is now the most successful auction site in the world and a household name. Plenty of people even make a living selling goods online, although they tend to sell in a specialised area like antiques or collectables, and are highly knowledgeable about their subject. But you don't need to be a specialist to make some decent cash, and eBay has estimated that the 'junk' sitting around in an average loft gathering dust could be sold for over £400.

To give you an idea of how much money is spent online, it's been shown that an item of women's clothing is sold every three seconds for an average price of £10, a pair of women's shoes is sold every ten seconds for an average price of £13, and a mobile phone is sold every sixteen seconds for an average price of £40. It's free to list items for sale, so have a good rummage through your wardrobes, cupboards, car boot and shed, arm yourself with a digital camera and start making some extra cash.

Ten steps to becoming a successful eBay seller

1. *Open an account.* Click on the 'sellers' link at the top of every eBay page, then click on to 'Create a seller's account' and fill in your details. For identification purposes you will be asked for your credit/debit card details and bank account details.

2. *Do your research.* Take a good look around the site and become familiar with the categories. Check what items have sold and for how much. You are not allowed to sell train or plane tickets, alcohol or tobacco on eBay, so avoid listing such items or your account will be closed.

3. *Get organised.* Having done your research, decide what items you want to sell (clothes, shoes, phones, books, jewellery) and divide them into boxes. Stock up on boxes, envelopes and any other packaging so you can dispatch the goods quickly as soon as you have a buyer.

4. *Choose between a fixed-price or auction listing.* There are two ways of selling on eBay – you can sell either at a fixed price (listed as 'buy it now') or at an auction. You need feedback from at least ten sales to create a fixed price listing, so if you are a brand new seller you will have to start with auction listings. It is now free to auction items with a 99p start price for a duration of up to ten days.

5. *Create your listing.* Write a clear, accurate – but eye-catching – description of your item. Be sure to include all the essential details, such as colour, measurements, condition and age of the item, and list factual details upfront – for example, 'size 10 Dolce & Gabbana blue jeans in good condition' rather than 'hip designer blue jeans'.

6. *Include photos.* You will generate several times more interest for your items if you include clear digital photos. Show any defects clearly and also consider taking photos of the item from different angles.

7. *Price it.* Having done your research decide how to price your item. Start low, especially if you are creating an auction listing and are new to selling online. You will also need to quote a price for postage and packing. The Post Office's website has a dedicated section for eBay users to help give an accurate costing. You will also have to decide on the duration of your listing. You can list an item for up to ten days, and it's a good idea to time this so that it includes a couple of weekends so that you attract the maximum number of bidders.

8. *Open a PayPal account.* The safest and most efficient way to buy and sell online is through a PayPal account (www.paypal.co.uk). This is a secure online payment service that enables you to make transactions without sharing any personal financial information. Money is credited to your PayPal account as soon as the purchase is made, and you can either withdraw this into your bank account or keep it in your PayPal account to make purchases. PayPal also operates a 'seller protection policy', which covers you against unauthorised payments, claims, charge-backs and reversals.

9. *Manage and complete the sale.* Use the online tool 'My eBay' to keep track of your sales. Once the listing ends, contact the successful buyer to arrange payment and delivery of the item. Do not dispatch the item until you have received payment and the funds have cleared.

10. *Leave feedback.* After receiving payment, leave feedback for your buyer, package the item carefully, dispatch it quickly to their delivery address and encourage them to leave feedback for you.

Where to stash your saved cash

By the end of this month you should have saved a significant amount on your weekly shopping bills and leisure activities. You may also be making some extra cash from eBay, and the small lifestyle changes you have made in the way you use your home will be contributing savings to your next utility bills. You will also notice how much money you save by avoiding impulse purchases at the January sales and in the supermarket. Now it's time to make the money you have saved work harder for you, so you can fulfil your financial dreams, so turn to Quick Reference 1 at the end of the book for ideas on how to save and invest your money.

File your tax return!

File your tax return by 31 January or you'll be hit with a £100 fine and charged interest on any money due.

2 February

February is the shortest month of the year, which means that pay day comes around that little bit quicker. As you will quickly discover as you work through the 12-month money-saving programme, you will find the greatest savings on everything from household sundries and clothes to weddings and even property if you go against the herd and shop 'out of season'. February is a great month to pick up bargains on summer items, such as garden furniture, barbecues and ice buckets. Winter is often a lean time for builders and contractors, so if you are looking to build an extension, install a loft conversion, or have a new kitchen or bathroom fitted, you may be able to negotiate a better price than if you wait till spring or summer.

Shrove Tuesday, which often falls in February, marks the day before Lent, a period of reflection and preparation before the joyful celebrations of Easter. Traditionally, Christians surrender a 'vice' such as chocolate or alcohol during Lent, and this can present a great money-saving opportunity. For example, if you give up a large daily cappuccino and forgo a couple of bottles of wine a week for the 40 days till Easter, you'll save yourself almost £170!

On a more cheerful note, Valentine's Day also falls in February (and almost always before Lent). Perhaps making a homemade card is a money-saving tip too far, but rustling up a romantic hamper at home will save you a fortune in inflated restaurant prices, and you won't have to drive home. If you do decide to eat out, you can save tens of pounds by taking a bottle of champagne or wine to a BYO restaurant (see p. 26).

In February many of us start making plans for a summer holiday.

It's generally far cheaper to take a family holiday during the May half-term than in late July or August, and now is a good time to book. If you really want to go away during the school summer holiday months but avoid peak season prices, why not consider a house swap? Full details on how to organise a successful house swap are given in the August chapter, but it does take several months to find a suitable fellow swapper and organise the exchange, so now is a good time to start browsing some of the websites and post your advertisement.

Although the days start lengthening in February, it still tends to be a cold and dreary month, and if you find yourself stuck in the office during your lunch breaks you might want to earn some extra cash by filling in a few online surveys. Survey sites pay you for your opinions, and the surveys, which take about 20 minutes to complete, can be quite fun. You can earn up to £200 a year if you become a regular survey-goer.

Food shopping

In the last chapter we showed how big supermarkets design their aisle and shelf layouts to entice you to spend more than you really need to and suggested ways in which you can beat the marketers at their own game. This month we give you the low-down on continental discount supermarkets, such as Lidl and Aldi.

Cut your supermarket bill in half

The German supermarkets Lidl and Aldi are a fantastic boon to money-savers. Unlike the large British supermarkets, they are no-frills stores that concentrate on selling good quality produce without fancy packaging, lighting, in-store music, deli counters and bakeries. Neither store accepts credit cards, and nor do they dish out free carrier bags at the checkouts. Such cost-cutting strategies mean they can pass on greater savings to the consumer.

Lidl and Aldi source produce such as cold meats, cheeses and confectionary directly from continental suppliers, with the result that you frequently get excellent quality food for at least a third less than at British supermarkets, and quite often you can save up to 75 per cent. For example, in one week in June 2010 you could pick up a large bag of fresh spinach in Lidl for 29p, whereas a similar bag in Tesco cost £1.89.

Unlike British supermarkets, Lidl and Aldi refrain from changing their store layouts every few weeks, which makes it easier and quicker to complete your weekly shop. In Lidl, for example, water, canned foods, fresh fruit and vegetables are usually stocked in the first aisles; chilled foods are along the back of the store; bread, cakes, biscuits, chocolates teas and coffees are in the middle; and alcohol and household sundries can be found in the last aisle.

Foods in season this month

Cabbage, celeriac, chicory, guinea fowl and halibut.

Storing cabbages: Wrap them up well in a plastic bag or clingfilm to keep them crisp, as cabbages lose moisture quickly.

Storing chicory: Chicory (often called endive in the US) is a popular vegetable in the Netherlands. It has a pure white colour, but light causes the leaves to turn green, so store chicory in a paper bag in the fridge, to keep it fresh for up to a week.

Be store-cupboard savvy

Well-organised kitchen cupboards are vital for money-saving cooks. Most of us clean out our cupboards once or twice a year and end up discarding armfuls of outdated spices, sauces and tinned foods that we bought on impulse. But just a few key ingredients – such as tinned tomatoes, beans or condensed milk – can form the basis for a tasty family meal that will cost just a couple of pounds to put together. Capers, anchovies, peppers and sun-dried tomatoes can also transform dishes made from leftovers. So set aside a couple of hours to make sure your food cupboards are appropriately stocked and efficiently organised.

If you have room, organise your store-cupboard foods by categories – baking ingredients; oils, spices and herbs; pasta, rice and couscous; pulses and lentils; tinned beans and vegetables; fish and meat. Place items that you use every day, such as pasta, lentils, oils and herbs, near the cooker and towards the front of the cupboard. Store foods that you use just occasionally – baking ingredients, perhaps, or seasonal foods, such as cranberries and mince meat – on the top shelf or at the back.

How to stock your kitchen cupboards for less

- Buy basic ingredients such as muesli, breakfast cereals, tinned tomatoes, lentils and tuna, and add your own dried fruits and nuts, herbs, sweetcorn and seasonings. Many brands inflate prices by as much as 40 per cent just for adding a handful of herbs, croutons and fancy fruits. Sweetened cereals such as frosted cornflakes are not only bad for children's teeth but can cost 50 per cent more than plain cornflakes.

- Avoid condiments and sauces in rustic-looking jars and don't buy store-cupboard staples, such as sea salt, that are packaged in smart boxes. They may look appealing, but you will get less for your money than if you buy a plain or 'basic' packaged product. Money-saving shoppers pay for ingredients, not the packages they come in.

- If you cook lots of stir-fries, curries and fajitas stock up on staples such as basmati rice, lentils, spices, noodles and sauces at local ethnic stores rather than a supermarket. They will be a lot cheaper, and there will be more choice.

- Buy small amounts of whole spices and grind them yourself. Whole spices last longer than ground ones and will taste fresher.

What the 'best before' dates really mean

'Best before' dates have recently come in for a lot of criticism from environmental campaigners, who believe that we are throwing away millions of pounds' worth of perfectly good food in the fear that it is unsafe to eat. The Food Standards Agency (FSA) currently uses three different labels to advise on the freshness and safety of foods:

- Use by – the FSA advises us not to consume foods after their 'use by' date. However, you can extend the life of many such foods by freezing them (see below). Follow the storage instructions, such as 'keep refrigerated' or 'consume within 48 hours of opening', on foods with a 'use by' date.

- Best before – this date refers to the quality of food rather than its safety, except when it comes to eggs. Never consume eggs that have passed their 'best before' date because they may contain salmonella bacteria, which could start to multiply after this date. However, you will not put your health at risk by consuming other foods that are past their 'best before' date. They may not be quite at their best, but they will not kill you.

- Display until/Sell by – these labels often appear next to foods with a 'best before' or 'use by' date. They are, in fact, used to alert shop staff not customers, so such foods are perfectly safe to buy and eat. Foods that have reached their 'sell by' date are often substantially reduced in price towards the end of the day.

The Approved Food website, www.approvedfood.co.uk, lists foods and drinks that have officially passed their 'sell by' date but not gone off, which is a great way to profit from the nanny state!

Invest in a freezer

A freezer is an excellent investment, especially if you have a family, as it will enable you to make significant savings by buying meat, bread and other perishable staples in bulk, and by freezing double quantities of homemade meals. If you plan to freeze a wide range of foods an upright freezer with shelves and compartments will be easier to organise than a chest freezer. It may be tempting to get carried away and buy the biggest freezer you can find, but bear in mind that a smaller freezer will be much cheaper and easier to manage. Follow our guide below to freezing food safely.

- *Prevent freezer burn.* Wrap food carefully before freezing it to exclude as much air as possible. This is particularly important with meat, because if it is 'burned' by the freezer ice it will become dry and tasteless.

- *Use up foods with strong flavours quickly.* Salt, spices and chillies intensify in flavour when they are frozen. The fibres of meat, fish and poultry also begin to break down, so foods such as smoked bacon and salted butter will have a shorter freezer life than unsmoked and unsalted varieties.

- *Don't throw it away.* There is no need to throw away foods that are kept in the freezer beyond their recommended time for fear that they will become unsafe to eat. Food that is properly frozen will not go bad – although its texture and taste will deteriorate over time. Make sure that you thoroughly thaw and cook any frozen food that is past the recommended 'use by' date.

- *Do not refreeze meats, poultry or cooked foods.* If you allow cooked dishes, meat or poultry to defrost (or they thaw during a power cut), it is not safe to refreeze them. They should be cooked thoroughly and consumed immediately or discarded. It is safe to refreeze thawed bread, cakes and pastry, but they will quickly become stale on rethawing.

- *Keep the freezer full.* An empty freezer uses much more power than a full one.

Should you freeze it?

It is not always clear which foods will freeze safely and successfully. As a rule, however, if you are in any doubt, freeze only those foods that have been cooked so that all the bacteria in meat and some of the enzymes in fruit and vegetables have been thoroughly destroyed.

Foods that freeze well

Raspberries; skimmed and semi-skimmed milk; double cream; eggs that have been lightly stirred or separated; spinach; potatoes (fully cooked or blanched in hot oil); fresh meat, poultry, fish and shellfish; creamy desserts, such as mousses, soufflés and cheesecakes set with gelatine, woody herbs, such as thyme and rosemary, and fresh root ginger.

What not to freeze

Whole melons and bananas; full-fat milk; cottage cheese; eggs in their shells; lettuce; uncooked potatoes; previously frozen uncooked meat, poultry, fish and shellfish; fruit jellies; and fresh egg custards.

Make double quantities

Make double quantities of your favourite soups, pasta sauces, stews and casseroles, pour them into sturdy margarine tubs and freeze them, so you always have a selection of ready-made home-cooked meals to hand. As a guide, a 1kg container stores the perfect amount of sauce for 500g of pasta. If you are freezing smaller amounts, remember that liquid expands as it freezes, so don't overfill containers.

Scrape the leftovers

The last dredges of a tasty gravy or sauce, a glug of wine or a spoonful of cream can transform a last-minute dish put together with leftovers, so get into the habit of scraping the pan and freezing the last bits of sauce, wine and cream in ice cube trays. Breadcrumbs will keep indefinitely in the freezer, so whiz up the ends of stale bread and store them in an airtight container.

Plan your summer holiday now

Now is the time to plan your summer holiday. Taking your family holiday during the May half-term rather than in August can save you up to £1,200 – enough for another holiday! Check the price comparison sites below to find the best deals on flights and hotels:

Flights

- www.kayak.com
- www.skyscanner.net
- www.flycheapo.com

Hotels

- www.trivago.com
- www.hotelly.com – states whether tax is included in the quoted room price and has videos of over half the hotels featured
- www.hotelscombined.com

Tackle DIY jobs

If you're planning to move house this year now is the time to start attending to all those niggling little DIY jobs. Fixing loose handles and cupboard doors, scrubbing up grotty tiles, filling in cracks in walls and ceilings, and giving the front door a quick lick of paint could add up to £5,000 onto the eventual sale price. Even if you are not planning to sell, keeping your home in good order will save you hundreds of pounds on home maintenance and insurance bills in the long run.

Stop door hinges from squeaking
A hinge that squeaks every time the door moves can be irritating. Put some petroleum jelly on the hinge pins to stop ill-timed noises.

Unstick stiff furniture drawers
Lubricate a sticky drawer by rubbing the bottom of the drawer and the supports on which it rests with a bar of soap.

Clean greasy hands with olive oil and sugar
After tackling all those dirty DIY jobs, get rid of grease and grime on your hands by pouring equal amounts of olive oil and sugar into the cupped palm of one hand and gently rubbing your hands together for several minutes. The grit of the sugar acts as an abrasive, while the oil helps to remove grease, paint and grime.

Sweeten the smell of your home
Your home can begin to feel a little fusty in deep winter with the central heating on full blast and the oven in constant use. To sweeten the smell of your sitting room, dab a couple of drops of vanilla extract on your light bulbs. The vanilla will heat up when you switch the lights on and fill the house with the delicious scent of fresh baking.

Remedies and treatments

Beauty treatments

If you're suffering from dry winter skin, treat yourself to a luscious homemade moisturiser.

Dry hair conditioner
Hair can feel particularly dry in winter when the central heating is on. Give a natural shine to dry, tired-looking locks by adding 1 litre of warm, unsweetened tea – instant will work as well as fresh brewed – to the final rinse after washing.

Foot moisturiser

To give tired feet a pick-me-up, rub shampoo over them before you go to bed and put on a light pair of socks. When you wake up your feet will be as soft and silky as they would if you'd treated them to an expensive pedicure.

Home remedies

Most of us suffer from a sniffle or two in winter. Buy own-brand aspirins, flu remedies and painkillers at the supermarket rather than leading brands. In late 2010 a packet of Sainsbury's aspirins cost 31p, compared with the leading brand, which cost £1.29. Instead of reaching for the cough mixture, you could also try soothing a sore throat or stuffy nose with one of the following homemade tonics.

Ginger tea

Bring a saucepan full of freshly grated ginger, lemon juice, crushed garlic and water to boil and allow to simmer for 20 minutes, adding honey to taste. The honey will soothe your throat, lemon is packed with vitamin C, and the ginger and garlic will help open your chest and nasal passages.

Lemon cayenne throat soother

Mix honey with lemon juice and a dash of cayenne pepper. The honey and lemon will coat your throat, while the cayenne pepper will help fight off infection.

Hot tomato gargle mixture

For temporary relief from a sore throat try a hot tomato gargle. Mix together a small glass of tomato juice with a small glass of hot (not boiling) water and add several drops of hot pepper sauce.

Valentine's Day

In recent years, as society has become increasingly commercialised, Valentine's Day has become a multimillion-pound industry for card retailers, florists, restaurants, hotels and gift shops. However, there are ways of trimming the cost without losing the romance.

Flowers

You can expect to pay a hefty premium to have a pre-ordered bouquet of red roses delivered to your loved one on Valentine's Day morning. In 2010 a dozen red roses ordered from Interflora would have set you back £39.99 plus an extra £12.99 for morning delivery. By contrast, you could pick up a dozen fresh red roses from a supermarket for less than £10. Alternatively, you can select a bunch of flowers from a local garden centre and put together your own bouquet.

Dining out

Many hotels and restaurants offer special deals on Valentine's Day. In 2010 www.toptable.co.uk had over 1,200 special offers for 14 February compared with fewer than 400 offers just two years before. It is also worth scouring www.lastminute.com for special deals, which have included special 'eat out for a tenner' and 'eat out for under £15' deals. If you fancy something more upmarket try www.viewlondon.co.uk. In 2010 it offered a three-course dinner at Harrods Georgian Restaurant for £35 a person – a real bargain given that a main course there can cost up to £40.

Eating in

If you don't want the stress of trying to rustle up a delicious romantic meal yourself, why not try one of the ready-made dine-in offers from one of the upmarket supermarkets such as Marks & Spencer or Waitrose.

Or put together your own special hamper (see June for some ideas) and enjoy an evening in with your favourite DVD.

Pancake Day, Lent and Easter

Pancakes were traditionally eaten on Shrove Tuesday because they are made with milk, flour and eggs – foods that were forbidden during the 40 days of Lent. Celebrate Shrove Tuesday with a pancake feast, using up scraps of sweet and savoury foods to make delicious fillings. You can make extra light and fluffy pancakes by substituting half the quantity of milk with sparkling mineral water.

Lent savings

Ditch the daily cappuccino
Do you nip into Starbucks on your way to work each day? Ditching the daily cappuccino habit will save you over £800 a year. If you really can't face the commute without a caffeine fix invest in a BiTE card from www.bitecards.co.uk, which will give you 20 per cent off food and drink bought at railway stations. That'll give you a saving of over £150 a year. Costa Coffee also offers a plastic loyalty card that allows you to view your balance online.

Get fit and lose weight
Gyms, health and slimming clubs vie for new members in January and February by offering discount joining fees. You don't need them. Get fit for free by walking instead of using your car, taking the stairs instead of the lift, going for a quick run round the park in your lunch hour and replacing takeaways with homemade meals. Many gyms and fitness clubs offer free trials, so if you really feel that you need a quick-fix workout, sign up for a handful of these.

Save on Easter chocolates

Chocolate shops usually run sales after Christmas, Easter and Valentines Day, so late February is a great time to stock up on chocolates for Mother's Day and Easter. Online chocolate retailers the Chocolate Trading Company (www.chocolatetradingco.com) and Hotel Chocolat (www.hotelchocolat.co.uk) often discount stock they want to clear quickly by up to 40 per cent. If you are a chocolate aficionado, the highly regarded Chocolate Society offers free membership and a 10 per cent discount on online purchases from www.chocolate.co.uk, as well as exclusive promotions.

Earn by doing online surveys

Survey sites pay for your opinions on everything from celebrities to public services, and completing an online survey is a fun and easy way to make some extra cash during your lunch hour. You will earn anything between 10p and £3 per survey, and each takes between 10 seconds and 30 minutes to complete. You are remunerated through vouchers for high street or online stores, such as Topshop and Amazon. However, you need to reach a certain threshold before they pay out, so work out how many surveys you will need to complete before you can actually cash in on your efforts.

How to make money from online surveys

- Set up a dedicated e-mail account to receive surveys.

- Sign up to several sites but never pay to register. There are numerous sites that require you to pay a registration fee of £80 on the promise that they will credit your account with £100 after completing your first survey; such sites are usually unscrupulous.

- Before you start completing a survey check how long it will take to complete and whether it is worth the reward. If you quit halfway through you won't earn anything. Some surveys will screen you out as ineligible after completing a few questions, which can be frustrating.

- Cash in as soon as you reach the threshold rather than 'saving up' all your points for a rainy day. Online money-making schemes like this are fast-moving businesses, and you never know when they'll move the goal posts.

Top online survey sites

- www.valuedopinions.co.uk – pays between £1 and £5 a survey in vouchers. The typical time to complete each is 10–30 minutes and the payment threshold is £10.

- www.onepoll.com – has speedy surveys on fun subjects. It pays 5–10p a survey, and each takes from 10 seconds to 2 minutes to complete. There is a high threshold of £40, and it pays an instant £2.50 when you sign up.

- www.lightspeedpanel.com

- www.globaltestmarket.com

Get paid to shop

If you love shopping and are finding your new money-saving regime a bit tough going, you might want to consider getting paid to indulge in a little retail therapy. There are numerous companies that will pay you for your opinions, and many dedicated mystery shoppers earn £300–400 a year for their efforts. It is also worth keeping an eye on your favourite department stores – Selfridges, for example, has its own mystery shopping panel.

Top mystery shopping sites

- www.retaileyes.co.uk
- www.tnsglobal.com
- www.sarosresearch.com
- www.mystery-shoppers.co.uk

3 March

The clocks go forward in March, marking the beginning of spring. As the days lengthen and homeware shops, DIY retailers and garden centres start filling their stores with colourful plants and shrubs, furniture and fabrics, most of us feel the urge to dust off the winter cobwebs and give our homes and wardrobes a good spring clean. However, filling your trolley with cans of abrasive bleaches, oven cleaners and furniture waxes is not just harmful to the environment (and possibly your own health) but will also burn a hole in your wallet. Instead, arm yourself with an extra large bottle of cheap white vinegar, a tub of bicarbonate of soda, some lemon juice and a few scented oils, and you will have your home fragrant and gleaming for a fraction of the cost. If you are looking to make home improvements but lack the necessary skills to do a professional job, why not see if you can swap skills with someone who has a talent for DIY?

High street fashion shops fill their windows and rails with eye-catching displays of the new season's clothes in March, but remember that fashion is not only fickle but also cyclical and increasingly versatile. If you take advantage of designer fashion ranges at supermarkets and discount chains, scout around market stalls and charity shops, and swap and customise old clothes you can revamp your spring wardrobe with designer clothes and quirky vintages for about a quarter of what you would spend in high street stores.

This month we also look at rewards cards. Research shows that about 85 per cent of UK households have at least one reward card; the giant in the field is the Tesco Clubcard. In 2010 the scheme had 15 million active members, who received £529 million in vouchers. The Clubcard offers great savings on family days out, so if you have a young family and haven't already signed up, now is a good time to do so to build up points for the summer.

Finally, if your son or daughter is hoping to go to university this autumn, turn to the June chapter for advice on how to apply for student finance. If you need to apply for a student loan for tuition fees and living expenses but do not need to supply additional 'evidence' for a maintenance grant, the deadline for completed applications usually falls sometime in early April to make sure that finance is in place by the start of the course, so now would be a good time to think about what you will need to do.

Food shopping

Foods in season this month

Early rhubarb, purple-sprouting broccoli, radishes, spinach and sorrel.

Storing broccoli: To stop it going mouldy, wrap broccoli in kitchen paper before putting it in an airtight bag.

Choosing and storing spinach: Look for fresh, tender leaves with a vibrant, deep green colour and no signs on yellowing on the stems. Avoid leaves that are slimy, wilted or bruised. Loosely packed in a plastic bag, the leaves should stay fresh for up to five days.

Perfect portions

Knowing exactly how many potatoes to roast or how much pasta to cook for a midweek supper for two or a Sunday lunch for eight can be tricky. Instead of estimating and making too much (or too little), log on to. www.lovefoodhatewaste.com for a 'perfect portion calculator'. For example, to cook a meal of roast chicken and new potatoes for a family for two adults and two children you would need 16 small potatoes and 480g of chicken.

Homemade cleaning products

To give your house a thorough spring clean, start upstairs and vacuum and dust rooms from back to front so that you bring the dirt down with you. The following homemade cleaning products will get your house fresh and gleaming in no time.

Clear out cobwebs
Cover your broom with an old pillowcase to clear out cobwebs in the corners of ceilings. It will stop the bristles of the broom from scratching the paintwork, and it is also much easier to remove cobwebs from a cloth than to pull them from the bristles.

Get rid of carpet odours
To get rid of pet smells sprinkle bicarbonate of soda on to carpets before vacuuming.

Windows and mirrors
Fill a plastic spray bottle with half hot water and half white vinegar, squirt on to mirrors and windows and buff them up till they sparkle.

The lavatory
Pour a large bottle of cola into the toilet bowl, let sit for an hour and flush for a sparkling clean finish.

Baths and taps
A squirt of shampoo is great for removing soap scum on baths and taps because it rinses clean.

Limescale
Soak pads of cotton wool in vinegar and wrap them around shower heads, taps and bath rims and any other areas on which limescale has built up. Leave for 30 minutes and the limescale should wipe away easily.

Cracks and crevices

To get rid of dirt and grime in hard-to-reach cracks and crevices, dip a toothpick or cocktail stick into some clear alcohol, such as gin, and rub it on to the affected areas. You can also use this to get rid of dust around the buttons of your phone and computer keyboard.

The oven

Add a teaspoonful of bicarbonate of soda to a cup of hot water, and use to get rid of oven grime. To remove baked-on food from oven plates, sprinkle the lumps of food with salt, dampen the area and let sit until it starts to lift the baked-on food, then simply wash away with hot soapy water.

The fridge

Put a couple of teaspoons of bicarbonate of soda on a saucer or in a small jar at the back of your fridge to get rid of odours. To get rid of stronger smells wipe the inside walls with a few drops of vanilla extract. To prolong the scent, soak a cotton wool ball or piece of sponge with vanilla extract and place it in the back of the fridge.

Deodorise the microwave

Vanilla extract will also get rid of fishy or spicy smells lurking in your microwave. Pour a little into a bowl and microwave it at a high setting for a minute to get rid of any residual odours.

Eliminate smells from frying fish

If you love cooking fresh fish but hate the smell that lingers around the house afterwards, add a dollop of peanut butter to your pan when you are frying fish. The peanut butter will absorb the odour instead of your carpets and curtains.

Woodwork

Add a drop of lemon juice to some olive oil to polish wood and leather sofas. Remove watermarks from wooden table tops by applying petroleum jelly around the marks and letting it sit overnight. The marks should wipe away with the jelly in the morning. Squeeze a blob of petroleum jelly on to chewing gum that is stuck on furniture legs or underneath tables to help remove the offending lumps.

Clean narrow-necked vases
Cleaning flower vases can be tricky. If the neck of the vase is too narrow for your hand, put a little sand and warm soapy water into the vase and swish it round gently. The sand will clean the residue inside.

Keep cut flowers fresh
Mix 3tbsp sugar and 2tbsp white wine vinegar into warm water and add this to your vase. Make sure that the cut stems are covered by at least 7cm of the mixture before you top up with water. The sugar will nourish the plants, and the vinegar will inhibit bacterial growth.

Preserve winter woollies
Good woollen clothing can last a lifetime if you keep the moths away. Fill drawstring muslin bags with sachets of cloves and place these in an unsealed plastic bag which will prevent oils or colour from transferring to the clothes. Attach plastic bags to the hangers of woollen items, or tuck one into your chest of drawers, to keep moths away.

Get chewing gum out of hair
If your child comes home from school with chewing gum stuck in their hair, try soaking the hair in a bowl of cola for a few minutes before rinsing it out.

Save on your spring wardrobe

Spending a fortune on up-to-the minute designer trends that last only a couple of months is not in keeping with the new age of the 'recessionista'. Indeed, customising clothes you bought a decade ago and putting together entire new outfits for less than £5 has become a badge of honour. A survey by Cami Confidential, a fashion label that designs clothes for women with breast cancer, found that more than a quarter of women have held on to a favourite item of clothing they bought more than a decade ago, and a third of women own at least one item of clothing that cost less than 50p.

You can source some fabulous fashion gems for less than half price at factory outlets and discount chains, and, of course, charity shops and market stalls are a popular stomping ground for bargain hunters. There are also burgeoning online fashion communities where you can swap dresses, shoes, bags and accessories. And if you're a little wary of trading used clothes online, why not organise your own swap-shop party?

Charity shops and market stalls

If you are prepared to rummage through the rails, you can pick up some great fashion buys at charity shops such as those run by Oxfam, the British Heart Foundation, Save the Children and Age Concern. Charity shops in affluent neighbourhoods of London and in smart towns and cities throughout the country are often great hunting grounds for designer bargains, especially around Christmas and after the summer season of regattas and races. Markets often specialise in vintage, designer and alternative fashions, and although they are not always cheap it is perfectly acceptable to haggle for a better discount, especially towards the end of the day.

Tips for buying second-hand clothes

- *Check for difficult stains.* If a garment is stained, assess whether it can be removed using a specialist detergent or by taking it to a specialist dry cleaner. Delicate fabrics, such as silk, can be difficult to treat, and colours and decorations on some fabrics can run and ruin the garment if they are machine-washed.

- *Remember that repairs can be costly.* It is easy enough to shorten dresses and skirts, repair fraying hems and replace buttons, but a garment that has holes or requires alteration around the shoulders or waist area will be trickier and more costly to repair or customise.

- *Know your rights.* Second-hand goods bought from market stalls, charity shops or online are covered by the Sale of Goods Act. This means that although you should expect some imperfections, the garments must be of satisfactory quality and fit for the purpose for which they were sold.

Top online second-hand clothes shops

- www.oxfam.org.uk/fashion – Oxfam has a fantastic online shopping site, where you can shop for vintage clothes according to decade and pick up second-hand celebrity clothes and accessories, donated by the likes of Annie Lennox, Shirley Bassey and Elle Macpherson. Oxfam also has seven boutique stores in London, Durham and Cardiff, and if you take a bag of unwanted Marks & Spencer clothes or soft furnishings into any Oxfam shop you'll get a voucher giving you £5 off when you spend £35 or more in M&S on clothing, homeware or beauty products.

- www.devotedtovintage.co.uk – a cheap and cheerful vintage emporium offering next day delivery and a full refund on unsuitable goods.

- www.youlovefashion.com – an online noticeboard for vintage and sample sales.

Factory outlets

You can save up to 75 per cent on the price of designer and high street brands by shopping at the retailer's discount outlet or by visiting a discount shopping centre, such as Bicester Village, where several outlets are gathered together under one roof.

Tips for shopping at discount outlets

- *Know exactly what you want.* As with supermarket shopping, arm yourself with a list of items you really want for that season, such as a new raincoat or pair of jeans. Do your research by checking stores and their websites, because the more specific you are, the less likely you are to waste money on unsuitable and impulse purchases.

- *Check the quality.* Check items carefully for missing buttons and loose hems and stitching, and look for make-up stains, especially around necklines.

- *Be clear about returns policies.* You may be travelling some distance to shop at a discount outlet so be clear about the shop's returns policy before you buy.

Top designer outlet and factory stores

Designer factory stores

- Burberry Factory Store (Hackney, London)

- Clark's Village (Street, Somerset)

- Laura Ashley Discount Shops (Hornsea, North Humberside; Newtown, Powys; Taplow, Buckinghamshire; and Thurrock, Essex)

- Mulberry Factory Shop (near Bath, Somerset)

- Aquascutum Factory Shop (Corby, Northamptonshire)

Factory store shopping malls

- Bicester Village, Oxfordshire (www.bicestervillage.com) – offers up to 60 per cent discount on 130 luxury boutique names, including Armani, Boden, Calvin Klein, Dolce & Gabbana, Jimmy Choo and Versace.

- The Galleria Outlet Centre, Hatfield, Hertfordshire (www.thegalleria.co.uk) – sells everything from fashion to books, homewares, toys and food.

- The Original Factory Shop, nationwide outlets (www.the originalfactoryshop.co.uk) – stocks discounted clothing, sportswear, electrical goods, homeware, toys and gifts at discounted prices. Many of its stores are located in small towns, offering easy access to elderly people and those without cars.

- Peak Village Outlet, Rowsley, Derbyshire (www.peak village.co.uk) – offers up to 30 per cent off the recommended retail prices on brands such as Cotton Traders, Pavers Shoes, Pringle and Hawkshead.

Discount chains

Discount chains such as Matalan and Primark sell designer clothes and homeware products at budget prices.

Matalan

This retailer was founded in 1985 and now has 300 stores across the UK, mainly in out-of-town locations. The stores have four sections – womenswear, menswear, childrenswear and homeware – and since 2006 the chain has added various 'shop in shop' sections offering a diverse range of high-quality brands. These have included Et Vous (high-quality womenswear), Sports Shop (offering brands such as PGA Tour and Umbro), Lee Cooper (casual menswear), 24/7 (casual menswear designed by Jeff Banks) and Influence (stylish but affordable home accessories by designers such as Antony Worrall Thompson, Gina D'Acampo and Linda Barker).

TK Maxx

This is the place to pick up designer clothes, accessories and household goods for up to 60 per cent less than their recommended retail prices.

You need to be prepared to rummage through the rails, but the stores are spacious and light, and you can make big savings on genuine designer clothes, including jeans, cashmere sweaters, dresses and shirts.

Primark

The Irish retailer, which has 139 stores across the UK, is renowned for selling on-trend fashions at budget prices. All merchandise is created specially for the chain. Primark makes savings by sourcing materials cheaply and buying in bulk, making clothes in simple designs and fabrics in the most popular sizes, and refraining from advertising. As well as clothes, Primark sells accessories, footwear, and health and beauty products.

Designer ranges at supermarkets

Supermarket chains are stealing a march on high street fashion shops with clothing ranges designed by big-name fashion designers at budget prices, and on everyday classic items, such as white shirts, sportswear and school uniforms, you can save up to 90 per cent on department store prices.

Tesco

In 2009 Tesco become the first supermarket to launch its own online fashion store, www.clothingattesco.com, in addition to stocking clothes in its stores. Brands include Florence & Fred Couture (a catwalk-inspired, fashion-forward collection of womenswear), Mischa Barton handbags, Cherokee menswear and My Favourite Things (a collection of childrenswear).

Asda

In 1990 Asda launched George, a range of high-quality, affordable clothes named after its designer George Davies, founder of fashion chain Next. Mintel estimates that George is now the fourth largest clothes retailer in the UK, after Marks & Spencer, the Arcadia Group and Next. The George label also includes dresses for brides and bridesmaids.

Sainsbury's

Sainsbury's entered the fashion fray in 1994 with its own brand TU, designed by Jeff Banks. It is aimed at 25–40-year-olds, and has made the supermarket into the eleventh largest clothing retailer in the UK, overtaking Topshop.

Swap clothes

The site www.bigwardrobe.com purports to be the largest online clothes swapping community and home to £1million worth of free clothes, bags and shoes. Another great site is www.whatsmineisyours.co.uk, which was founded in 1994 by stylist and personal shopper Judy Berger. Also check out the Freecycle Network at www.freecycle.org, which allows you to give away stuff and replace it with new things for free.

Make your own clothes

Sewing machine sales have rocketed in the past couple of years as more of us are embracing the 'make-do-and-mend' philosophy. You can pick up a good quality machine for around £50 from a reputable retailer such as John Lewis, and there are numerous websites giving advice on stitching techniques, fabrics and measurements, and free patterns to get you started. The online sewing directory Freeneedle provides links to free sewing tutorials, patterns and projects, and Burda and Simplicity produce dressmaking patterns that are popular with beginners.

Market stalls are great places to look for cheap fabrics, and Fabrics-n-stuff sells fabrics starting at 99p a metre. Abakhan is also recommended by craft lovers, and it has nine shops located in the north-west of England as well as an online shop.

Of course, you do not have to sew to make a new outfit. Customising old clothes is very much in vogue, and you can create an infinite number of different looks by cutting, ripping, dying, embellishing, shortening and lengthening clothes, adding a belt or new buttons, on experimenting with different decorations.

Top sites for making your own clothes

- www.fabrics-n-stuff.co.uk
- www.abakhan.co.uk
- www.freeneedle.com
- www.burda.com
- www.simplicity.com

Rewards cards

Tesco launched its Clubcard in 1995, and a year later research revealed that Clubcard holders were spending 28 per cent more at Tesco and 16 per cent less at Sainsbury's than before, so the rival supermarket launched its own rewards card – Nectar. Many partners have since signed up to the Nectar scheme, and you can collect points at BP garages, Homebase and several websites, including Amazon.

Not all supermarkets have jumped on the rewards card bandwagon. Asda has steered clear of the market, claiming that the money it would have spent on marketing and administering a card scheme is used instead to cut prices.

As well the two supermarkets, the Co-op offers its customers a dividend card, and Boots and Waterstones have their own rewards cards. Coffee shops and restaurants are also joining in on the act – in April 2010, for example, Costa Coffee launched a plastic loyalty card.

Tips for making loyalty cards pay

- Sign up for all loyalty cards, but shop in a store only if it offers the best value for money, not solely for the points.

- Do look out for genuine savings. A three-for-two on your favourite brand of toothpaste at Boots may, for example, be a better bet than paying full price for an own-brand product at a supermarket.

- Do log on to the card websites regularly to check your points balance and for any updates on new opportunities to collect points. For example, Nectar often offers double points at BP garages and getting the saving couldn't be simpler: simply click on the offer and it is automatically uploaded on to your card.

Top loyalty cards

- Sainsbury's Nectar card – points for every £1 spent in store, online and at Sainsbury's petrol stations and Homebase. Every 500 points gives you £2.50 to spend in store, or at Argos, Vue cinemas, the travel site www.expedia.co.uk, Eurostar and on Philips electrical goods. The points are worth double at Legoland, Thorpe Park and Alton Towers and Chessington World of Adventures, and Ask restaurants.

- Tesco Clubcard – 2 points for every £1 spent in store and online at Tesco and 1 point on every £1 spent at Tesco petrol stations. When you have collected 150 points you will be given a £1.50 voucher.

- Boots Advantage Card – 4 points for every £1 pound spent. Each point is worth 1p.

- Waterstones – 3 points for every £1 spent.

- Costa Coffee – 5 points for every £1 spent. Each point is worth 1p and can be redeemed against food and drink purchased from Costa Coffee shops.

4 April

April is one of the most important months in the financial calendar because the end of the tax year falls at the beginning of month – the personal tax year runs from 6 April to 5 April of the following year. To understand why, we need to go back to the Middle Ages, when Britain followed the Julian calendar, made up of quarters. The first day of each 'quarter' fell on four religious festivals that fell close to the two solstices (24 June, Midsummer's Day, and 25 December, Christmas) and two equinoxes (25 March, Lady Day, and 29 September, Michaelmas). It was on these first 'quarter' days that servants were hired, payroll services processed and rents paid.

Until 1752 Lady Day on 25 March also marked the start of the New Year, so it made sense for the financial year to follow suit. In 1752, when the Julian calendar was replaced by the Gregorian calendar, it was discovered that these two calendars were out of step by 11 days (due to the different ways in which leap years were accounted for). The tax authorities felt it was unacceptable to lose 11 days' tax revenue, so the start of the tax year was moved to 5 April. In 1800 the start of the tax year shifted again to 6 April due to the leap day being 'skipped' in the Julian calendar, and it has remained so ever since. University terms still follow quarter days, and rents on some business premises are still due on quarter days, but otherwise quarter days hold little significance.

The 18th-century American politician Benjamin Franklin said: 'We can be certain of nothing in life expect death and taxes.' Indeed, we are taxed on just about everything: we pay VAT on nearly all goods and services, income tax on our earnings, capital gains tax on profits over a certain limit on stocks, shares and assets such as investment properties, stamp duty on property and, of course, inheritance tax if you are lucky enough to have been bequeathed an estate worth more than the inheritance tax threshold, but unfortunate enough to have benefactors who failed to plan for it.

There are many legitimate ways to avoid paying taxes. This chapter cannot cover complex issues such as capital gains tax and inheritance tax in detail, and if you own assets, such as investment properties or a large estate that is likely to trigger tax liabilities, the best money-saving action you can take is to obtain specialist advice. Failure to do so could cost you or your beneficiaries hundreds of thousands of pounds, wiping away any money savings you may make from this book.

As well as taxing our income and assets, the government also pays out to those in receipt of low or moderate incomes, in the form of tax credits. The tax credit system is complicated and like all other state benefits was cut in the coalition budget of June 2010. However, if you care for young children, have a disability or earn less than £20,000 per annum it is worth applying for tax credits, which could boost your income by hundreds of pounds a year.

On a more cheerful note, Easter also tends to fall sometime in April, so when you've finished tax saving, indulge in some homemade chocolate treats. The Easter weekend is also a good time to get out into the garden and start growing your own fruit and vegetables, and composting your food waste.

Food shopping

Foods in season this month

Cockles, kale, morel mushrooms, spring lamb and wild garlic.

Choosing and storing mushrooms: Look for mushrooms that are firm, plump and clean and that have a creamy white colour, as mushrooms darken with age. To preserve their moisture without allowing them to become soggy, wrap mushrooms in a damp cloth and store them in a loosely closed brown paper bag.

Choosing and storing garlic: Select plump garlic heads with unbroken skins and avoid garlic that is soft or shrivelled or has begun to sprout. It is not essential to store garlic in the fridge, but do keep it in a cool, dark place where it is not exposed to heat and light. Whole bulbs will keep fresh for up to two months, but their lifespan shortens once broken up into cloves.

Swap and barter your skills

You can save a fortune on everything from DIY jobs around the house to specialist legal advice, music lessons and beauty treatments by swapping skills. The idea of exchanging goods and services has been steadily gaining momentum in the past couple of years and www.swapaskill.com has over 10,000 members who offer everything from freshly caught fish to professional photography, French lessons and accountancy services. Another site that advertises skills is www.gumtree.com.

A countrywide network of local community bartering schemes has also been flourishing for several years. Local Exchange and Trading schemes (LETS) allow members to exchange goods and services. Log on to www.letslinkuk.net for details.

Grow your own fruit and vegetables

An iceberg lettuce and a packet of cherry tomatoes can easily set you back more than £2 at a supermarket; by far the most cost-effective, tasty and satisfying way of getting your five-a-day portions of fruit and vegetables is to grow your own. As I'm sure you've heard numerous times before, you do not need a large garden or allotment to cultivate a kitchen garden: a sunny windowsill or balcony is all that is needed to grow a number of herbs and salad leaves.

Herbs
Basil, chives, parsley, mint, coriander, sage and oregano can be grown on a sunny windowsill, and will save you a fortune on shop-bought

packets of dried herbs. Rosemary is a fairly hardy shrub that will survive cold weather and can be left outside all year round, even when it is in a container. If you are not confident enough to grow from seed, you can pick up a pot-grown plant in a supermarket or garden centre for just over £1. As long as you keep the plants watered and make sure they get enough sunlight, they will produce tasty leaves until the early autumn. Freshly picked herbs can transform salads, fish and meat dishes, pasta dishes, sauces, omelettes, sandwiches and dips.

Vegetables

Lettuce, spinach, radishes, potatoes, tomatoes, chillies, peppers, carrots and courgettes can be grown in containers on patios or balconies, and they will provide a colourful display as well as a culinary delight.

Fruit

Strawberries and blueberries can be grown in hanging baskets or containers on a sunny patio. Any extra fruit can be sold at summer fetes, made into delicious summer puddings and desserts or boiled up to make jams and fruit sauces.

Getting started

All you need to get started on your kitchen garden are some containers and compost. Later in the season you will also need a plant fertiliser. So that there is sufficient room for your produce to grow, use containers that measure at least 23–25 centimetres across. Plastic containers are cheaper, lighter and less prone to drying out than terracotta containers. To grow potatoes, however, you will need deep containers or special potato-growing bags.

Tomatoes and strawberries can be grown in hanging baskets, making them easier to harvest as well as creating attractive displays. Plant your seeds in new, good quality compost at the beginning of the season. After about five weeks, you should start applying a good liquid feed, and then continue feeding throughout the growing season. It is best to feed plants in the evening, especially in hot weather, because the water is less likely to evaporate.

You are also likely to need to some pest control. A vegetable insecticide spray should keep flies and caterpillars at bay, while netting will stop birds, rabbits and mice nibbling away at your produce.

Protect vegetables with spare tyres

April can bring changeable weather that can quickly destroy young plants and shrubs, so if you have room consider planting tomatoes, potatoes, aubergines, peppers and other vegetables inside old car tyres laid on the ground. The deep rim of the tyres protects the vegetables and shrubs from harsh winds in early spring, while the dark rubber will absorb heat from the sun and warmth from the surrounding soil.

Compost your food waste

Composting turns your kitchen and garden waste into valuable, nutrient-rich food for your garden. Almost half the food waste you would normally throw away can be turned into compost, which can be used to improve the condition of your garden soil and to feed your flowers, fruit and vegetables.

Get a cut-price compost bin

A compost bin from a hardware store costs about £40, but many local councils sell plastic bins for a quarter of the price, and they may even throw in a free kitchen caddie in which to keep vegetable peelings, teabags and eggshells. It takes from nine months to a year for compost to become ready for use, but composting works faster in warm weather, so you will see the contents breaking down more rapidly if you start in early spring. For more information log on to www.recyclenow.com.

Let your house to a film or TV company

Film and television production companies are always on the lookout for homes that can be used as location sets for films, TV dramas, commercials, documentaries and photo shoots. All types of properties are required – from bedsits to Victorian terraced houses, smart contemporary conversions and classic period homes. It helps if you have big rooms and ample parking space outside your property, as production companies tend to come with lots of crew members and bulky pieces of equipment.

If you can cope with the disruption you can earn anything from £250 a day for a photo shoot to more than £3,000 if your home is used as a film or TV set. Companies will pay for any breakages, but if they are filming for more than one day you may need to move out of your property altogether. The agencies in the box below specialise in matching properties with production companies, and if you happen to live in the type of abode they are looking for, it could be a great money-spinner.

Top location agencies

- Lavish Locations: www.lavishlocations.com

- Film Locations UK: www.locations-uk.com

- Sarah Eastell Locations: www.film-locations.co.uk

- BBC Locations Department: 0208 225 9133

Tax credits

Tax credits are state benefit payments that provide extra income to working families with children, disabled people and workers on a low income. There are, at present, two types of tax credit: Working Tax

Credits and Child Tax Credits. Credits are means tested, but you do not necessarily have to be paying tax or making National Insurance contributions to qualify, and you can ask for payments to be made directly into your bank account.

The tax credit system is complex and convoluted. Following the changes made in June 2010, the system is also far less generous than it was, particularly for families that fall in the middle-income bracket of £25,000–£40,000.

Payments are based on your personal circumstances and income in the *previous tax year* (which runs from 6 April to 5 April the next year). So, if you make a claim on 20 April 2012 it will be based on income earned between 6 April 2011 and 5 April 2012. If you are married or living with a partner you must make a joint tax credit claim, and both your incomes will be taken into account.

Apply early

Tax credit payments can be backdated for a maximum of three months only, so apply as soon as you think you may be eligible. For example, if you had a baby on 1 March but HM Revenue & Customs (HMRC) did not receive your claim form until 1 December, you would receive credits only from 1 September.

You can protect your tax credits by applying early, which is especially helpful if you think your income may fall. For example, if you know your income is currently too high to be eligible for tax credits but you may be made redundant on 10 October, you should still make a claim for credits on 6 April. You will receive an award notice informing you that you will not be paid credits because your income is too high. However, if you are made redundant on 10 October and you contact HMRC again with an estimate of your lower income for the year, you may be entitled to tax credits from 6 April. If you leave it until 10 October to make a claim, your credit would be backdated to 10 July.

Working Tax Credits

Working Tax Credits are top-up payments to help people on low incomes, people with a disability and families with children but to be eligible you must work at least 16 hours a week. The Working Tax Credit is made of several different 'elements' or payments, and the amount you receive depends on which elements you are eligible for; lone parents or people with a disability may receive more money. The Working Tax Credit also includes an element for working families that spend money on approved childcare. Parents can claim 80 per cent of childcare costs up to a maximum of £175 a week for one child and £300 for two or more children.

From April 2011 families with an income of more than £40,000 will no longer be eligible for Working Tax Credits. On the other hand, families earning £40,000 or less will be able to claim a total of £545 a year in Working Tax Credits for the tax year 2011–12. The following year, in April 2012, families earning up to £25,000 can claim a maximum of £460 in tax credits, but those earning above this threshold will see their entitlement drop to nil. However, families with an income of less than £20,000 will see their entitlement increase slightly.

Child Tax Credits

If you are responsible for at least one child or young person you may be able to claim Child Tax Credits. Like Working Tax Credits, Child Tax Credits are made up of different elements, but unlike Working Tax Credits you do not have to be working to claim them.

Both Working Tax Credit and Child Tax Credit rates increase each year, but as of April 2011 the increases will be linked to the Consumer Price Index (CPI) rather than the Retail Prices Index (RPI). The CPI tends to rise at a lower rate than the RPI, so the increases will be less generous than in previous years. Those in receipt of Child Tax Credits will receive an extra £150 on top of these rate increases.

> ## Contacts for advice about tax credits
>
> - Tax Credit Helpline: 0845 300 3900
> - www.taxcredits.hmrc.gov.uk
> - www.adviceguide.org.uk

Capital gains tax

If you have a second home, let properties or own stocks and shares, you may have to pay capital gains tax (CGT) when you sell these assets (if the profit is over the annual allowance). The CGT allowance for individuals for the tax year 2010–11 is £10,100, and everything above this is taxed at one of two rates, basic rate taxpayers at 18 per cent and higher rate taxpayers at 28 per cent.

If you own two properties you can decide which to classify as a second home for capital gains tax purposes. It does not have to be your main residence, so it makes sense to classify the property with the higher value as your 'second' property.

Inheritance tax

Inheritance tax (also known as 'death duty') is paid by anyone who inherits an estate valued over the inheritance tax threshold. For the tax year 2010–11 the threshold was £325,000, and everything above that amount was taxed at 40 per cent. However, since October 2007 couples have been allowed to transfer their allowance to their spouse on their death. In effect, this change doubled the inheritance tax threshold for most couples, because when the first spouse dies they simply transfer their £325,000 to the surviving spouse. Unless a couple's estate is valued over £650,000, therefore, they are unlikely to leave their heirs with an inheritance tax liability.

However, even if your estate is valued at considerably more than your inheritance tax threshold(s), there are legitimate ways in which you can avoid passing on an inheritance tax bill to your children or heirs. There are two basic ways of doing this: you can 'beat' the inheritance tax trap by gifting chunks of your estate or you can 'meet' it by taking out insurances to meet the tax bill. Whichever route you pursue, it is vital to take advice from a solicitor and tax adviser specialising in the area, and it is also essential to make a will. Far too many families trigger inheritance tax liabilities simply because they bury their heads in the sand rather than confronting the issue before it is too late. Not for nothing is it said that 'inheritance tax is only a problem for those who distrust their heirs more than they dislike the Inland Revenue'.

Check your council tax

Don't forget to check that your property is in the correct council tax band by logging on to the Valuation Office Agency website (www.voa.gov.uk). Enter your postcode and house number to see which band you fall into, then do the same with your neighbour's number to check that they are not paying less than you.

5 May

May is the only month in the year when we enjoy two bank holidays, and families with young children often want to make the most of these long spring weekends with days out to theme parks, zoos or stately homes. Government research carried out in early 2010 found that, in these cash-strapped times, a week-long holiday is no longer considered an essential staple of family life and that many families are choosing to replace their annual holiday with days out or long weekend breaks.

However, a family day pass to a popular theme park can easily set you back £200, so this is where Tesco Clubcard vouchers and online discount vouchers really come into their own. As we explain again in the August chapter, you will reap four times the value of your Clubcard points on days out tokens than you would on shopping in store – a £5 Clubcard voucher can be exchanged for £20 worth of discount tokens at theme parks, wildlife centres and other attractions around the country. All you have to do is log on to the website and select the attraction you want to visit; you will receive your tokens in the post within five working days.

If you do want a family holiday in the sun, May is the month in which to do it, and the discount website www.savoo.co.uk found that travel companies offer the greatest discounts on holidays in May. Of course, it is not just the cost of the holiday itself. Extras such as airport parking, car hire, bank charges and commission on foreign currency, travel insurance and roaming mobile phone costs can burn a severe hole in your pocket, so follow our guide to getting the best deals on these items.

May is traditionally also the prime time for moving house, espe-cially for families who want to be settled into a new home before the start of the new school year in September. If you are thinking of moving, find out how to sell your home yourself instead of using an estate agent – it could save you thousands of pounds in commission.

Finally, as you look forward to midsummer and the longest day of the year, do you really need 500 TV channels? Ditch the satellite TV subscription and take advantage of the lighter evenings.

Food shopping

Foods in season this month

Asparagus, cherries, elderflower, Jersey Royal new potatoes, mint, spring onions, sweetcorn and watercress.

Choosing and storing asparagus: St George's Day on 23 April marks the official start of the short asparagus season. British asparagus is considered the world's finest, but it is an expensive delicacy, so visit one of the many farms across the UK where you can pick your own. Look for stalks that are rounded, not twisted, and stems that are firm and thin. Select closed tips that are deep green or purplish in colour – purple tips will have a fruitier flavour. Store asparagus with the ends wrapped in a damp paper towel, at the back of the fridge, as the folate is destroyed by exposure to heat, air and light. The spears are best consumed within two days of purchase.

Storing potatoes: If you buy potatoes in bulk, or grow your own, add an apple to the sack to prevent them from flowering.

Protect fledging plants from insects

As the weather becomes warmer there's nothing more frustrating than a swarm of insects nibbling at fledging green shoots. Mix a handful of black pepper with some flour and sprinkle it around your plants to keep ants, aphids and earwigs away.

Take an early summer holiday

Research by Santander Cards found that some tour operators inflate prices on package holidays by more than 80 per cent in late July and August. Recent government guidelines mean parents can be penalised or even prosecuted for withdrawing their children from school for holidays without good reason, so if you want to take advantage of lower prices and fewer crowds (and less sunburn), take your family summer holiday during this month's half-term. Discount website www.savoo.co.uk found that some travel firms slash their prices by up to 55 per cent in May. Follow our guide so that you get the best deal on all the extras too.

Travel money

Don't buy foreign currency at the airport

Always order your foreign currency in advance – you will get a much better exchange rate and pay less commission. The Consumers' Association magazine *Which?* found that the airport branches of Travelex, TTT and American Express provided the worst value for money for exchanging currency. If you had exchanged £100 at the Moneycorp kiosk at Gatwick's North Terminal in July 2010 you'd have got just £107 worth of euros, but if you had ordered your euros online from the International Currency Exchange (ICE) and collected them from Waterloo Station you'd have got nearly £118 worth. Remember that the Post Office and Marks & Spencer offer commission-free currency.

Don't withdraw cash on your credit card

If you withdraw cash on your credit card while you are abroad, you'll be stung with a triple whammy of fees: a hidden foreign exchange fee, an ATM withdrawal fee and interest from day one. On the most expensive cards, such as American Express, First Direct, HSBC and MBNA, withdrawing £100 abroad could end up costing you a total of £110.

Beware of debit card charges

Avoid using your debit card to withdraw cash or make multiple small purchases for drinks and gifts. The most expensive banks, such as Barclays and NatWest, charge up to £4.75 for a £100 cash withdrawal and a charge of between £1 and £1.50 each time you use the card to make a purchase, and this is on top of the foreign exchange fee. A handful of cards offer commission-free cash withdrawals in some parts of the world. Santander's Zero credit card has no foreign currency loading, for example – and others worth considering are those offered by Saga and the Post Office.

Don't ask for the bill to be converted into sterling

Many restaurants, shops and hotels, especially in Southern Europe, will offer to convert your bill into sterling. Do not accept, as you will be given a very poor exchange rate. If the bill is converted automatically, refuse the reversed transaction and ask to pay in the local currency.

Tell your bank before you go abroad

Banks are becoming increasingly cautious about overseas credit and debit card activity, so inform them of your travel plans before you go. In addition, make sure to give your bank a 24-hour contact number for you abroad, so that if your card is blocked they can contact you quickly and rectify the problem. If you incur extra costs such as taxi fares and phone calls to reactivate your card, you should ask your bank to reimburse you when you get home.

Airport parking

Save up to 30 per cent on the cost of airport parking by booking your space in advance. Look at www.save-on-parking.co.uk, which offers a choice of up to 80 different car parks at 25 UK airports.

Car hire

Car hire firms often double their rental charges in popular European hotspots during peak holiday times, and many also use scare tactics to frighten you into buying more insurance than you need. When you're searching for a car be flexible about which model you hire – hire charges on popular small cars can be £200 more than on larger cars. Use a comparison site such as www.kayak.co.uk to search for the best value rentals, or www.carrentals.co.uk, which compares rental costs in both the UK and abroad.

Fill up the petrol tank

Read the small print carefully if you hire a car abroad. Most require you to return the car with a full tank of petrol or pay well over the odds for the firm to refill it themselves. You may be offered the opportunity to use a car with a full tank of fuel and return it with an empty tank for a small fee, but this is likely to cost you twice as much as if you'd filled it up yourself.

Watch out for insurance cover scams

All car rental companies charge an excess when drivers have had an accident, and this can be as much as £1,000. They will allow you to lower the excess for an extra charge, but this can substantially increase your bill for a minor bump or scrape. Do not be lured into buying extra insurances that may already be covered elsewhere. The website www.dailyexcess.com provides insurance to protect motorists from steep excess charges when they are driving abroad. For £4.75 a day, you can buy cover against excess charges worldwide when you are renting a car for a period of ten days or less. Policies include damage to windows, tyres, the undercarriage and the roof, which is often excluded from alternative policies. And if you are taking your own car overseas check what cover your policy offers abroad and make sure you have international breakdown cover.

Mobile phones

Making and receiving just a handful of mobile phone calls while on holiday abroad can result in an eye-watering bill when you get home. For example, O_2 charges £1.37 to make a call home from the USA, and £1.03 to receive a call. Avoid using your mobile to access the internet abroad – costs can be exorbitant.

The best way to keep costs down is to text. Texts are free to receive, and from Europe usually cost around 11p to send, or between 25p and 40p from countries further afield.

Travel insurance

The cheapest travel insurance is not always the best. Check the small print on the policy carefully before you buy, to make sure that you have sufficient cover. In particular beware of the following points:

- *Medical cover.* Be sure to inform your insurer if you are (or a member of your party is) taking medication; many insurers will try to wriggle out of paying expensive medical bills claims if they were not given relevant information upfront. A minimum of £2 million medical cover is advisable.

- *Cancellation cover.* If you book your holiday independently, make sure you have sufficient cover for flights, hotels and car hire.

- *Cash and baggage.* Ensure your cash is covered and that you are also protected if your baggage is lost or stolen. Carry essential medication in your hand luggage. Personal liability cover of £1 million is advised.

- *Delays, holiday abandonment/curtailment.* Many cheaper policies don't include delays. Always keep receipts for accommodation, emergency car hire and food. If you are delayed, request a confirmation letter from your airline to support your claim.

Get a free European Health Insurance card from www.ehic.org.uk. This entitles you to free or reduced medical treatment anywhere in the

European Union, Iceland, Switzerland and Norway, and travel insurers may waive their excess if you use it to get treatment.

Sell your house without an estate agent

May is a popular month for house selling and buying. Estate agents may charge as much as 3 per cent of the agreed sale price in commission to sell your home, but the growth of private-sale property websites, such as www.houseladder.co.uk, means it has never been easier to sell your home yourself. Follow our five-point plan to cutting out the estate agent and avoiding their commission – on a sale of a £250,000 house, it could save you as much as £7,250.

1. *Set a price.* Invite two or three estate agents to provide a free valuation for your home – you do not have to tell them that you are planning to sell privately. Also look on property sites such as www.rightmove.co.uk and www.findaproperty.com for similar properties in your area that are for sale. It is worth monitoring these sites and keeping a watch on property sales in your area a few months before put your own home up for sale. If a number of properties similar to yours have been on the market for several weeks, it might be worth under-cutting the price by £5,000. Log on to www.nethouseprices.com to find out what prices properties in your area have sold for.

2. *Get an energy efficiency graph.* To sell your home you will need an energy efficiency graph, which costs around £45. Even if you sell through an estate agent, order the graph yourself rather than through the agent as they will include a hidden commission in the quoted price.

3. *Prepare your marketing materials.* Private property websites such as www.propertybroker.co.uk and www.houseladder.co.uk will erect a 'For Sale' board outside your property and take

professional quality photographs, which you can then use to advertise your home. You will also need to provide them with a written description of the property. Spend time writing a detailed and accurate description that includes a brief description of the property itself ('ground floor garden flat', 'modern three-bed semi-detached house', 'Victorian terraced house', for example); the number of reception rooms, bedrooms and bathrooms; any fitted appliances in the kitchen; and whether the property has a garden, balcony, loft space, off-street parking or a garage. It is also worth giving a flavour of the local area and amenities – for example, if the property is a short walk from the train station or in the catchment area of well-regarded schools.

4. *Hold viewings.* When a prospective buyer contacts you to arrange a viewing make a note of their full name and contact details. You should also ask them if they have a property to sell themselves. When they come to view the house, you should be polite and businesslike as you show them around your home, but there is no need to be over-friendly. Take the viewing at their pace and avoid pointing out too many features at once.

5. *Negotiate offers carefully.* You will have to negotiate offers your self and make sure that the sale goes through to completion. Most buyers are canny enough to know that you will be saving the commission by selling your home yourself, and they will make a low offer in the hope that you will pass on some of these savings to them. Unless you are offered the full asking price (which is unlikely), express disappointment at the first offer and try to meet your buyer somewhere between, but don't haggle to death – this will only create bad feeling from the start.

Top property websites for selling your home

- www.thelittlehousecompany.co.uk
- www.houseweb.co.uk
- www.mypropertyforsale.co.uk
- www.propertybroker.co.uk

6 June

June is one of the most glorious months of the year, with clear blue skies, warm sunshine and long light evenings. It is also one of the busiest months for families that have young children, due to an abundance of school fetes, garden parties, festivals and carnivals. Such events can provide a great opportunity to make some extra cash by selling your own jams, pickles, cakes, crafts and hampers.

If you don't grow your own produce, why not try foraging for wild food? Mushrooms, wild garlic, nettles, elderflowers and berries grow in abundance between June and October, and they can be used to make delicious soups, cordials, omelettes and risottos. If you live near the coast, grab a bucket and net and go hunting for seaweed, cockles, mussels, crabs and even lobsters. But foraging for wild food (particularly mushrooms, which can be poisonous) requires some expertise and plant knowledge. Richard Mabey's *Food for Free* has been the leading guidebook on this subject since it was first published in 1972.

This is also the most popular month in the year for getting married. Weddings have a reputation for being expensive because everyone, from venue suppliers to caterers and photographers, hikes up their fees when they are asked to quote for the big day. The best money-saving advice is to get married on a weekday outside peak season, but it is possible to have a midsummer wedding on a Saturday afternoon while keeping to a reasonable budget, by avoiding expensive venues and other costly extras. The trick is to distinguish between the things that are really essential and those that won't make much difference on the day, and then to enlist as much help from friends and family as possible.

Youngsters taking GCSE and A level exams may find that June is a particularly stressful time. On top of their worries about exams, going to university has never been more expensive, with tuition fees likely to increase over the coming years, and, of course, a degree is no longer an automatic passport to a graduate job. But if the prospect of nursing thousands of pounds' worth of debt before you've even started earning is depressing, it is worth taking heart from Alvin Hall's aphorism: 'A good education is the one thing of value that can never be lost or stolen.'

Food shopping

Foods in season this month

Courgettes, elderflowers, gooseberries, grey mullet, lettuce, peas, peppers, raspberries, salmon and tayberries.

Storing lettuce: Wrap up well in plastic, and store in the crisper drawer. Revive limp leaves by placing them in a bowl of cold water with a few slices of peeled potato – they'll be as good as new.

Washing lettuce: This can be a bore. If you're preparing a big salad for a barbecue or dinner party, pull apart the lettuce leaves, throw them into a clean pillow case placed inside another case, close the end with a rubber band and put it into the washing machine with a large item such as a towel to balance out the load. Run the rinse and spin cycle; the leaves will be rinsed and dried far more thoroughly than if you'd used a salad spinner.

Make your own lunch

You've probably heard the advice time and time again: taking your own sandwiches into work instead of rushing out to the nearest sand-wich bar or café will save you a small fortune over the year. But there's an added incentive to do this in the warm summer months, when you can escape from your desk and enjoy your lunch in a nearby park.

Invest in a meat slicer

Cold meats are a delicious addition to any summer picnic, lunch or supper. Investing in a meat slicer can save you around 15 per cent when compared to the cost of buying pre-packed or deli-sliced hams, salamis, chorizo or garlic sausage. The unsliced meat will also stay fresher for longer.

Keep your kitchen free of flies

Flies are a perennial summer nuisance, but you can keep your kitchen free of them with a non-toxic homemade fly trap. Simmer 400ml milk, 110g raw sugar and 60g ground pepper in a saucepan for about 10 minutes, stirring occasionally. Pour the mixture into shallow bowls or saucers and place them around the kitchen and patio, or any other areas where flies are a problem. The flies will flock to the sugary bowls and drown in the sticky mixture rather than poisoning your food.

Pick your own fruit and vegetables

If you don't grow your own fruit and vegetables and are not confident enough to go foraging, the next best thing is to pick your own. A few hours spent gathering fresh strawberries or tomatoes can make a great family day out. The National Farmers' Retail and Markets Association (FARMA) represents farmers and producers working on a local scale who sell direct to the public at nearly 600 pick-your-own farms across the UK. See www.pickyourownfarms.org.uk for details of your nearest farm.

Summer school uniforms

Instead of forking out for shorts that will last only a couple of months, cut the bottoms of worn trousers and hem them.

Make your own hampers

Everyone loves a hamper, and they are one the easiest (but often most impressive) money-saving gifts to put together. If you've been following the advice so far in this book, you'll already have a stash of wrapping paper, ribbons, cards, bits of fabric, cellophane and other decorations. Grab a handful of cheap wicker baskets from a bargain shop like Poundland and make up a hamper to suit any taste or occasion. Food and drink hampers are the obvious choice, and the possibilities are endless: jams, homemade cookies and sweets, cheese and wine bought cheaply on a booze cruise (see p. 123), and pickles and condiments. But you can also experiment with other themes. Here are some suggestions to get you started:

- Pamper hamper – a pretty basket stuffed with luscious homemade beauty products will delight any teenage girl or woman.

- Arts and crafts hamper – put together a selection of coloured pens, papers, cardboards, glitter and glues to make a hamper for creative kids.

- Kitchen hamper – rustle up some cookie cutters, a rolling pin, apron and cake decorations to make a children's baking hamper.

- Garden hamper – a selection of seeds, a pair of gardening gloves and some pretty pots will delight anyone with green fingers.

Father's Day presents

Forget cufflinks, ties, golf clubs or the latest gadgets. One of the best free gifts you can give on Father's Day is a service voucher, so offer to cut the lawn, wash the car, tidy the garage or paint the garden fence.

Chic money-saving weddings

According to *Wedding* magazine, the average cost of a traditional wedding and a honeymoon in 2010 was £19,600. Caterers, reception venues, photographers, florists and stationers rub their hands in glee and hike up their fees when they are asked to quote a price for a couple's big day (it is not unknown for popular venues to add an extra zero to the hire cost). But big, glitzy *Hello*-style weddings are not really a sign of the times. With a little creative savvy and lots of help from friends and family, you can have a relaxed, fun, stylish and memorable wedding for just a few thousand pounds.

Set a budget

Professional wedding planners advise that the best way to control your budget for the big day is to decide how to divide it up. They recommend allocating half the budget to the cost of the service and reception, and splitting the remaining half among wedding attire (bride's dress, groom's outfit, bridesmaids' dresses, going-away outfits), flowers, photography, entertainment, stationery, thank-you gifts and other miscellaneous costs. Having decided on your budget, set up a dedicated bank account in which to deposit your funds and from which to pay expenses. This will discourage you from going over budget. Keep careful track of your spending by logging all expenditure on a spreadsheet.

The service

A no-frills ceremony at a Register Office will cost no more than £100, but a traditional church service, complete with choir, organist and bellringers, can cost almost £800. There are ways of keeping costs down, however – by arranging your own flowers, using the services of talented local music students, or forgoing the bellringing as the wedding congregation departs.

The reception

A Saturday afternoon reception in June will not only have to be booked at least a year in advance but could also cost twice as much as a Sunday or weekday wedding in quieter months such as January, March or November. However, if you do decide on a midsummer wedding there are ways of cutting the costs:

- *Limit the guest list.* Obviously the more people you invite the higher your catering bill will be, so consider inviting just close family and friends to the reception.

- *Have a buffet-style meal.* A buffet provides a relaxed ambience, and you will need fewer serving staff than for a sit-down meal. In addition, with a selection of foods to choose from it is easier to cater for vegetarians and others with special food requirements.

- *Provide your own booze.* You can make great savings by buying your own wines but do check the venue's corkage fees before you go down this route.

- *Serve sparkling wine.* Consider serving Prosecco or a good quality Cava instead of Champagne after the toast – few will notice the difference.

- *Employ local catering students.* Obviously students will be cheaper than using professional staff and chefs, and they may also bring some fresh culinary ideas.

The dress

Designer dresses may be well made but you're only going to wear your wedding dress once so you don't need to pay extra for durability. Few ready-made dresses fit perfectly, so to save on alteration costs look for a dress with a corset inside as it will be much easier and cheaper to alter. If you want to keep your dress after the big day, buy a wedding dress box from eBay to take along when you have it cleaned – professional cleaners can charge up to £150 for a box, on top of the cleaning costs.

Top charity shop bridal boutiques

Many charity stores now have bridal departments offering specialist advice on wedding dresses, accessories and bridesmaids' dresses.

- Oxfam (www.oxfam.org.uk) has bridal departments in eleven of its stores. Over 95 per cent of the dresses are new and have come from designers and bridal shops changing stock. Many are designer dresses in mint condition. The average cost of a dress in 2010 was £250, and Oxfam aims to save brides at least 30 per cent on high street prices.

- Barnados (www.bridesbyappointment.co.uk) has three bridal stores located in Shropshire, Edinburgh and London. None of its stock is pre-owned. They sell end-of-line products, generously donated by retailers and manufacturers, and claim you can save up to 80 per cent on the recommended retail price. Wedding gowns start at £90.

- The British Red Cross (www.redcross.org.uk) has a bridal store in Dorking.

Tips for buying second-hand wedding dresses

- Wedding dresses are bought to be worn only once, so brides will not care too much about stains or tears, especially after the service. Inspect the dress carefully and contact a specialist cleaner to confirm that any blemishes can be successfully removed.

- Make sure that the colour is exactly right, because this is something you cannot change.

The honeymoon

Research has shown that the average cost of a honeymoon is £3,000, but there are several ways to trim the cost or even to have the entire trip paid for in the form of wedding presents.

- *Upgrade for free.* Do inform hotels and airlines that you are on your honeymoon and they may give you an upgrade.

- *Get cashback.* Pay for your honeymoon and all expenses on a cash-back credit card.

- *Ask guests to contribute.* The award-winning travel agent Travel Counsellors (www.travelcounsellors.co.uk) offers a honeymoon gift registry, where guests can buy their wedding present in the form of a contribution to the honeymoon. Simply set up an account with them and they provide you with personalised cards to enclose with your invitations, explaining how to purchase a honeymoon contribution gift. The company will also send a thank-you card to every guest who contributes, and provide you with regular updates on your account balance.

Free entertainment

A pair of tickets at the Royal Opera House could set you back over £150. But in June and July you can catch relays of world-class ballet and opera performances for free at open air BP Big Screen viewings around the country. Pack a picnic, get there early to secure a good vantage spot and enjoy the festive atmosphere. Find your nearest screening by visiting the Royal Opera House website at www.roh.org.uk.

Student finances

A survey by the Association of Investment Companies found that the average student completing a three-year degree course in July 2011 will graduate with a debt of £21,198. For students attending a university in England and Wales the debts include tuition fees; Scottish students studying at Scottish universities do not have to pay tuition fees. During the academic year 2010–11 tuition fees were capped at £3,225 a year, but universities have long been campaigning to increase the cap to help fill the gaping hole in higher education funding, and it is likely that an increase will be seen in future years. Currently, undergraduate students can take out subsidised government loans to cover the cost of tuition fees and living expenses.

The abolition of free higher education means that many parents have had to resign themselves to making further sacrifices to fund their children's education. Research by the trust fund provider The Children's Mutual found that today's parents expect to spend more than £30,000 to help support their children between the ages of 18 and 30.

Apply for student finance

If you are a prospective student hoping to go to university this autumn who needs help paying tuition fees or living expenses, you should apply for student finance now. The deadline for new student applications generally falls around the third week in June to ensure that finance is in place for the start of the academic year in September, and although you can still apply after the June deadline, the money may not be available by the start of your course. There is no need to wait for a confirmed place before applying for finance – simply state your first choice on the application form, and advise the Student Loans Company if this changes later on.

There are three main sources of financial support for full-time students – student loans, maintenance grants and bursaries – and the good news is that you can apply for all three on a single application form. Full-time students embarking on undergraduate degrees are eligible for two loans: one for tuition fees (£3,290 for 2010–11) and a maintenance loan (up to £4,950 for students living away from home, in locations outside London).

Every student is entitled to a full loan for tuition fees and maintenance expenses, regardless of household income. Student Finance England pays tuition fees direct to the university or college.

Maintenance grants

If your family's annual household income is less than £50,000, you will also be eligible for a maintenance grant. If your household income is less than £25,000, you will be eligible for the full maintenance grant, which for the academic year 2010–11 was £2,906.

Bursaries

Students in receipt of a full maintenance grant are also entitled to a minimum bursary from their university or college. Many institutions will award more than the minimum bursary (£329 in the academic year 2010–11), and they may also award bursaries to students on partial maintenance grants.

Paying back the loans

You are currently only required to start paying back your student loans once you are earning over £15,000 a year. Interest is accrued on the loans at the rate of inflation, so in real terms you will pay back only the amount you borrowed.

Making an application

The following information is needed for your first application:

- Passport number
- National Insurance number
- Bank details
- The start date of your proposed course

See the website www.directgov.uk/studentfinance for more details.

7 July

July marks the beginning of the long school summer holidays, and for working parents finding affordable childcare for the six-week period can be a real headache. Most local authorities run holiday clubs and play schemes for school-aged children, but demand for places exceeds supply, especially in London, and many are booked up well in advance. The costs can also mount up if you rely on holiday clubs to keep your children occupied throughout the summer break. Research by the charity the Daycare Trust found that in 2010 the average cost of a week's childcare was £91; funding two school-aged children for the entire six-week summer holiday could, therefore, end up costing over £1,000.

Catering for children over the summer holidays can also become expensive if you rely on ready-made foods and snacks. Buying and cooking food in bulk, and freezing meals, snacks and sandwich fillings, will allow you to feed your children (and their friends) cheaply and healthily. The trick to feeding children and fridge-raiding teenagers on a budget over the summer holidays is to plan weekly menus around foods that are on offer in the supermarkets. So if whole chickens are on offer one week, for example, buy three or four and freeze the surplus. A roast chicken can obviously form one main meal, but if you buy a slightly larger bird you can turn the leftovers into chicken nuggets, salads, pasta dishes, pies and sandwiches. And, remember that it is always cheaper to buy a whole chicken than portions of legs and drumsticks, so if you are planning a barbecue, buy a whole bird and joint it at home.

Shops begin slashing their prices in earnest for the summer sales around mid-July, and clothes, accessories, shoes and electrical items are reduced by a much greater margin than in the January sales. Indeed, it is not uncommon to find stock reduced by as much as 70 per cent towards the end of month, so this is a good time to pick up items that may make good Christmas presents or stocking or hamper fillers.

Finally, if you claim tax credits you must renew your application by post or phone by 31 July or your payments may stop. This is particularly important from July 2011 onwards, because changes to the system mean that many families who previously received tax credits will no longer be entitled to benefits, and may even have to pay back over-payments.

Food shopping

Bulk buying

You can make huge savings by bulk-buying long-life groceries such as pasta, cooking oils, canned foods and household sundries at cash-and-carry stores. The cash-and-carry industry sells primarily to independent grocery stores and catering businesses, and stock is purchased with this clientele in mind, so goods are sold in the largest quantities and sizes. Cash-and-carry stores sell to trade members only and are not open to the general public, but some stores offer membership to professions outside retailing and catering or to local community groups, such as PTAs and playgroups. As the cash-and-carry stores supply to catering outlets, their meat, fish, cheeses and delicatessen foods tend to be of good quality.

Costco

Costco is a members-only cash and carry that offers trade membership (including a spouse's card) to catering and grocery trade customers for an annual fee of £20 plus VAT. Membership is also available to individuals who either work in (or are retired from) finance, local government, education, health, police and legal professions, and it also offers membership to some other professions. The non-trade membership fee is £25 plus VAT, and you will need proof of identity, a certificate of professional qualification and proof of address.

Makro UK
Makro, which offers membership to businesses only, requires copies of documents such as VAT registration, business invoices and proof of identity before it will issue a trade card.

Amazon
In 2010 established online retailer Amazon joined the likes of Tesco, Sainsbury's and Ocado by selling groceries and household sundries. It now sells over 22,000 brands, including Walkers, Kraft and Pampers, as well as gourmet foods from small local suppliers that are not available in mainstream supermarkets. You can make big savings by purchasing non-perishable goods in bulk, and standard delivery is free. Alternatively, for £49 a year you can sign up to Amazon Prime to get guaranteed next-day delivery.

Club together

Take advantage of cash-and-carry memberships by clubbing together with neighbours and other young families and shopping in bulk. It is also worth clubbing together to make salads, jams, ice creams, sandwich fillings and marinades in bulk.

Foods in season this month

Aubergines, blueberries, clams, fennel, loganberries, pike, pilchards, raspberries, sage, strawberries and tomatoes.

Choosing and storing aubergines: Look for smooth, well-rounded and symmetrical aubergines of a uniform colour. Heavier vegetables are best – lighter ones may taste woody. Medium-sized aubergines will be young, sweet and tender, but over-sized ones tend to be tough, seedy and bitter. Store them in a plastic bag in the fridge (the ideal temperature is 10°C), and they should keep fresh for up to four days. Aubergines are delicate vegetables, so be careful not to puncture or bruise them, as this causes them to rot.

Choosing and storing fennel: Fresh fennel will have a fragrant aroma. Look for bulbs that are firm and solid, with no signs of splitting, spotting or bruising. Those with whitish or pale green leaves are best, and avoid bulbs that show signs of flowering, which indicates a vegetable that is past its best. Fennel can be stored in the fridge for up to four days; however, as it ages it loses it flavour, so use it sooner rather than later.

Keeping cool

Homemade spritzers and ice lollies

Freeze leftover white wine in ice cube trays and add these to a glass of cold water to make a delicious spritzer. You can also freeze leftover fruit juices to make ice lollies for the kids. Freeze red wine and use it in sauces and stews.

Keep a jug of water in the fridge

Fill up a jug of tap water and put it in the fridge to chill so you always have chilled water on hand in the summer months. On average we waste about 10 litres of water a day just by running the tap while the water turns cold, which ends up costing nearly a £1 a month.

Organise a 'Big Lunch'

The Big Lunch was launched by the Eden Project in July 2009 in a bid to bring together people from different generations and backgrounds within a community. The idea is modelled on the great British street party. Basically, you cordon off a cul-de-sac or take over some public green space in your neighbourhood, and everyone chips in with chairs, tables, food, drink and music. It's a great way of getting to know your neighbours. Visit www.thebiglunch.com for more information.

Graduate accounts

Most students have sizeable debts when they graduate, but banks recognise that graduates are likely to earn more than non-graduates in the future, and are eager for graduate custom, so now is a good time to switch accounts if your current bank is not offering the best deal.

Many banks offer 'graduate accounts' that allow you to keep an interest-free overdraft for up to five years after you graduate, but you are expected to pay off the overdraft in tiered stages. For example, for the academic year 2010–11 Lloyds TSB was offering a three-year graduate account package with a £2,000 overdraft in the first year, reducing to £1,000 in the third year. It was also offering a free European flight voucher to new customers. Barclays was offering a generous five-year package with a £3,000 overdraft limit in the first year, reducing to £200 in the fifth. However, the bank levies a monthly fee of £7, so you effectively pay £84 a year for the 'free' overdraft facility.

If you are continuing your education with postgraduate study, Santander currently offers a four-year postgraduate account with an interest-free overdraft that begins at £1,000, increasing to £1,800 by the fourth year of postgraduate study. The websites www.moneyfacts.co.uk and www.moneysupermarket.com have comparison tables to help you find the best graduate account for your needs.

Free festivals

If you are a student you can get into summer festivals for free by working as a volunteer. Check out www.networkrecycling.co.uk for opportunities.

Car boot sales

Car boot sales are great places to sell things you can't sell online, or simply a way of giving your garage or loft a good clear out. People come to browse and pick up bargains, so keep your pricing simple and low – books, CDs, toys and children's clothes often start as low as 20p per item. It's a good idea to have at least two people manning each car boot so that you can keep an eye on both the goods and the takings. A couple of foldaway tables will be useful for displaying items. Make sure all your stock is clearly priced and labelled beforehand and take a good supply of plastic carrier bags and cardboard boxes for people to carry their goods home in.

Car boot sales are listed in local newspapers and on www.carboot junction.com. If you are simply selling unwanted goods as a one-off you do not have to pay tax, but if you become a trader (that is, you buy goods with the intention of selling them again), you are liable to pay income tax on your earnings.

Buy a bike

Save on fuel costs, and reduce your carbon footprint by getting out and about by bike. One of the best places to pick up a cheap bicycle is at a police auction, where unclaimed stolen bikes are sold off for a fraction of their retail price. Log on to www.bumblebeeauctions.co.uk to find the next police auction in your area.

Cut the cost of holiday childcare

Summer schools and private day camps can be great fun for school-aged children, but they are expensive for parents. Although there are many organisations that provide a fun-filled week of supervised activities for less than £100 a week, they usually get booked up quickly, so start researching what is available in your area well before the holiday period begins.

Holiday clubs and activities

Local authority schemes

Most local councils organise holiday play schemes throughout the summer holidays. They are run by qualified staff and offer a range of fun outdoor and indoor activities. Such schemes are ideal for working parents and, depending on the activities offered, can cost less than £100 a week.

Camps and courses

If your children belong to organisations such as the Brownies, Guides or Scouts, check if they run any outdoor camps, treks or courses over the summer holidays. Army, sea and air cadet groups also organise residential courses.

YMCA holiday activities

YMCAs around the country organise holiday and summer activities for children aged from 5 to 14, including sports, day trips and arts and crafts activities. They usually offer discounts for those who book early.

Sports activities

Most local sports and leisure centres put on a full programme of holiday activities for school-aged kids. These can range from week-long swimming or tennis courses to free half-day taster sessions of new sports, such as trampolining. Water centres also offer courses in sailing, canoeing and kayaking.

Theatre, arts and crafts

Local art galleries, museums, theatres, and dance and music groups usually offer interesting holiday activities such as drama classes, workshops that culminate in a performance, or even storytelling and puppet-making classes. Many churches also run holiday clubs for children, and local libraries may organise holiday reading clubs, as well as being a valuable source of information on what's on in your area.

Cheaper childcare

Even if you sign up your children for holiday clubs for a week or two, you will still need to organise care and keep them occupied for the rest of the holiday. Trainee nannies are often keen to gain experience and may offer their services at a lower rate than fully qualified nannies, while students and trainee teachers may also be able to offer low-cost childcare.

Share the care

The summer holidays are a great opportunity for grandparents and relatives to spend some quality time with their grandchildren, nephews and nieces. Club together with other family members who have school-aged children and share childcare over the summer months. You could also arrange to share the services of a nanny, au pair or childminder with other families in your area.

Holiday projects

It's a good idea to devise a large project to keep your children occupied and entertained over several weeks. Traditional outdoor activities, such as building dens or tree houses, are great fun. You could also give them a small plot in the garden in which to grow herbs, flowers and vegetables. Meanwhile, putting together a large scrapbook, painting a mural or making a patchwork quilt will keep artistic children entertained for hours.

Crafty cash

If your children or teenagers become bitten by the arts-and-crafts making bug and want to sell their creations, direct them towards www.etsy.com. This US-based online crafts mall has become *the* place to buy and sell everything from handmade clothes to bags, candles, jewellery and ceramics. It is also a fantastic place to find unusual gifts.

Only a small percentage of the site's registered members are also sellers, so it is a great place to showcase and profit from your talents.

End-of-summer sales

You can save up to 60 per cent on summer clothing if you wait until mid-July or August. Discount website www.savoo.co.uk found that you can also save up to 20 per cent on the cost of electrical goods and computers during July. Remember, online retailers also hold sales, and items that have not sold during the season are heavily discounted.

Renew your tax credit claim

If you are paid Working Tax or Child Tax Credits you must renew your claim by post or phone by 31 July or you may lose your payments. Call the tax credit helpline on 0845 300 3900.

8 August

August is the most relaxed month of the year even for those at work. The days are long and golden, schools and universities are closed, and the pace of life is slow. Most of us associate August with holidays, and the past four decades have seen an unprecedented growth in the number of Britons taking foreign summer holidays. However, the recession has placed the great British holiday firmly back on the agenda, and in 2009 the travel industry recorded the biggest annual fall in trips abroad since the 1970s, while the media coined a new term for holidaying at home – the 'staycation'.

There are numerous options for taking a cheap and enjoyable break in the UK, and camping and caravanning holidays have soared in popularity. Camping became popular as an outdoor adventure pursuit for Edwardian gentlemen at the turn of the 20th century, and it was the standard British family holiday in 1960s. However, the face of camping has changed considerably, and there is now a range of chic, upmarket options such as yurts and tipis. Indeed, it is possible to go camping with your hair straighteners and laptop if you really want, and this has led the media to coin a new term for this modern pursuit – 'glamping'.

August is also one of the busiest months in the year for the nation's roads, with an estimated 14 million cars heading off for family days out and vacations. You can reduce the cost of your summer motoring considerably by turning off the air conditioning when you're driving around town, by maintaining the correct tyre pressure, by searching for the cheapest petrol prices and by driving at a steady speed.

The last week of this month marks the final bank holiday in the year before Christmas, after which thoughts turn towards preparing for the new school term and the routine of work. Before shelling out on new school uniforms, see if you can restore last year's white shirts and sports kit with some old-fashioned home laundry tricks.

August can be an extremely hectic month for parents. If the crowds, noise and heat become too much, and you yearn for a low-cost recuperative break, why not escape to a retreat centre. Most centres have a religious affiliation, but they are open to all and offer comfortable accommodation, home-cooked food, and a bit of peace and quiet – all in a tranquil location.

Food shopping

Foods in season this month

Fruit and vegetables grow rampantly in August. Robust-flavoured Mediterranean vegetables such as aubergines, juicy tomatoes, courgettes, peppers and onions are in season, and are great for barbecues. Celery also comes into season in August. Raspberries, gooseberries, greengages, redcurrants and blackcurrants grow in abundance, and they make delicious jams and summer puddings. Nectarines and Victoria plums come into season towards the end of the month, and hedgerows start filling with blackberries. August marks the opening of the game season, and red mullet and sea bass from the Cornish waters are also at their best.

Storing fruit and vegetables: Store strong-smelling vegetables, such as leeks, onions and shallots, away from potatoes and fruit.

Cut the cost of summer motoring

If you have children you will probably be using your car much more during the summer holidays. Air conditioning, roof racks, underinflated tyres and overfilled boots can add several pounds to your fuel costs, so this summer make an effort to slash your motoring costs by changing the way you drive.

Save on MOT, repairs and maintenance

Take your car to your local council MOT centre rather than using a private garage. If you do resort to a private garage, choose Nationwide Autocentres (www.nationwideautocentres.co.uk) and use your Tesco Clubcard vouchers. A £2.50 voucher will knock £10 off your MOT bill.

Clean car windscreens with sparkling water

Keep a spray bottle filled with sparkling water in your car boot to remove grease and bird droppings from you windscreen. The fizzy water will help speed up the cleaning process. Sparkling water is also good for loosening rusty nuts and bolts.

Save on fuel

Reduce the load

Take unwanted goods out of your car boot and avoid driving around with a roof rack as these added loads increase aerodynamic drag and use up more fuel.

Turn off the air conditioning

Air conditioning uses an incredible amount of fuel when you are driving at slow speeds, so wind down the window and open the sunroof instead when driving around town. Conversely, having the windows down and opening the sunroof when you are driving at high speeds can reduce fuel efficiency by 10 per cent, as it increases drag and uses more fuel, so turn on the air conditioning when you're on the motorway. For day-to-day driving, *Autotrader* magazine reckons that you can save £2 a week by turning off the air conditioning.

Check your tyre pressure

Check your car's tyre pressure each week. *Autotrader* estimates that driving with under-inflated tyres can increase your fuel consumption by 5 per cent.

Reduce your speed

Driving at 85mph is not just illegal but also uses 25 per cent more fuel than driving at 70mph.

Pay less for petrol and parking

Log on to www.petrolprices.co.uk to search for the cheapest filling stations in your area and research parking costs in advance on www.youcanpark.com. If you drive to a station on a regular basis and have to pay for parking, it may be cheaper and easier to hire a permanent parking space from www.yourparkingspace.co.uk.

Cut the cost of a family day out

With a bit of forward planning you can make huge savings on days out that the whole family will enjoy. There are many ways you can cut the cost of days out this summer.

Use Clubcard points and discount vouchers

You will reap four times the value of your Tesco Clubcard points if you use them for days out rather than redeeming them against your shopping bill. Points can be exchanged for vouchers and tokens at museums, historic houses and castles, and at wildlife and theme parks. However, you will need to plan ahead. Log on to the Clubcard website, select your outing and call the venue, and you will be sent your free tickets in the post. Discount websites such as www.myvouchers.co.uk also offer a plethora of offers on family days out, so it is worth keeping a close eye on these sites too.

Travel for less

Get a family railcard

It is worth investing in a family railcard, as the initial cost will pay for itself in just a few trips. The card costs £24 a year, and you'll save a

third on most adult fares and 60 per cent on child fares. Log on to
www.railcard.co.uk for details of other promotions, such as free YHA
(Youth Hostelling Association) membership when you buy your
family railcard online.

Travel in London for free

Children under the age of 11 who live in London can travel for free
on the Tube, London overground trains and Docklands Light Railway
with a free Oyster Photocard (see www.tfe.gov.uk/oyster for details).
Children visiting the capital can also travel for free when accompanied
by an adult with a valid ticket.

Find the cheapest fares

Finding the cheapest way to make a train journey can be a minefield,
but there are websites that can help. You can travel along certain routes for just
£1 if you book early enough on www.megatrain.co.uk, and www.side
step.com searches over 200 travel websites to find you the cheapest fare.

Free theatre tickets

For the past 13 years Ticketmaster has been running Kidsweek,
a scheme that offers free tickets to top London shows and
activities to children aged from 5 to 16 who are accompanied
by at least one adult paying the full ticket price. In 2010 the
promotion ran for three weeks to meet the demand. See
www.kidsweek.co.uk for details.

Think ahead

If you are likely to visit the same popular attraction more than three
or four times a year it is worth buying an annual pass or membership.
For example, a single adult entry ticket to London Zoo costs £15.40,
whereas an annual pass costs £50 and you can visit as many times as
you like. Annual membership to the National Trust costs £46 and offers

free parking and entry to its 300 historic houses and gardens, many of which put on special events for children over the summer holidays. English Heritage maintains over 400 historic sites and its annual membership costs £41.50, allowing free entry to its castles, monuments and fine homes.

Buy family tickets online

You can also save money by buying family tickets to popular attractions – such as Legoland, Chessington World of Adventures, Thorpe Park and Alton Towers – online. For example, it would cost a family of four £123.34 to purchase four tickets on the day to Legoland, but this would come down £81.30 if the tickets were bought at least seven days in advance via the internet.

Organise a picnic

Freshen up your thermos flask

If you've just dug out the thermos flask for a picnic and find it smells a bit musty when you unscrew the cap, next time you store it away place a whole clove or teaspoon of salt inside before screwing the cap back on.

Beach hand cleanser

Add a plastic bag full of baby powder to your beach kit to get sand off your hands before eating. Simply rub your hands in the bag of powder and the sand will be gone, leaving you to enjoy grit-free sandwiches.

Stop fizzy drinks from going flat

If you can't finish a can of cola or lemonade in one go, place it in a large zip-lock plastic bag, which should keep the drink fizzy until you're thirsty again.

Stop wasps from ruining your picnic

There's nothing more annoying than wasps buzzing around while you're trying to enjoy a picnic or meal in the garden. Take along an old plastic container, fill it with water sweetened with sugar and cut a hole in the lid. The wasps will be attracted to the water, crawl inside and be unable to get out.

Summer health

Car sickness
Squirt a few drops of lavender oil on to some cotton wool balls, and put them in a sealable plastic bag. If someone is feeling car sick, a few whiffs of the lavender oil will calm them down and make them feel better.

Homemade suncare cream
For quick, temporary relief of mild sunburn, apply some plain natural yoghurt to the affected skin. This will give skin some much-needed moisture and, at the same time, the coolness of the yoghurt also acts as a soother. Leave it on for a few minutes, then rinse off with cold water.

Keep feet smelling sweet
Keep foot odours at bay by crumbling a couple of fresh sage leaves into your shoes, socks or tights before you put them on. Sage kills the bacteria that cause foot odour in warm, moist environments.

Take a staycation

In these times of austerity, the great British holiday is back in fashion, and if you really want to watch the pennies, it is possible to book a week's camping holiday for four that costs less than your family's weekly grocery shop.

Beach trips

No area of Britain is more than 80 kilometres from the coast, and a day at the beach is a great traditional family day out. The Marine

Conservation Society's website, www.goodbeachguide.co.uk, recommends beaches with the best water quality for safe bathing, and you can search for a beach by region or name. If you are looking for a bolthole on the sands in which to store your bathing suits, deckchairs and picnics, you might want to consider renting (or even buying) a beach hut.

The wooden beach hut started life as a changing room for modest sea-loving Edwardians, but its popularity has not abated. Huts are owned by private individuals (many have been passed down through the generations) and by local councils. There are often long waiting lists to rent a hut on popular beaches, especially along the south coast and Suffolk, and a hut on the right beach can prove to be an excellent investment. Some owners in Dorset have seen the value of their huts rise from £20,000 to £120,000, and large huts in popular locations can be let for over £1,000 a year.

Caravans and camper vans

Billy Butlin opened his first campsite in Skegness in 1938 in order to offer families a week's holiday for a week's pay. It was a great success, and by the 1960s hundreds of modern-looking, chalet-style holiday camps with swimming pools, bars, novelty attractions and organised entertainment had sprung up around the country. Bookings at caravan and self-catering holiday sites (such as Butlins) have soared by 30 per cent since the onslaught of the credit crunch; you can expect to grab a last-minute deal on a caravan that sleeps eight people for under £400 a week. If you like the idea of exploring the country with your own home on the road, consider renting a camper van, which is basically a vehicle that provides both transport and accommodation. Modern camper vans usually have a small kitchen, lavatory/shower facilities, beds that double up as daytime seating areas and extendable awnings. You can rent a 1960s-style camper van that sleeps a family of four for about £325 a week.

Camping

Camping holidays have surged in popularity in the past couple of years. A survey conducted in early 2010 by the retailer Halfords found that 50 per cent of British families were planning to go camping that summer, compared with just one in five in 2009. Camping holidays have undergone a real revolution in recent years; at the budget end of the market you can pitch a tent at a municipal site for under £10 a night but at the luxury end of the scale you will find swish family-friendly sites with smart, well-equipped bathrooms, play areas, cooking and food storage facilities.

You can pick up a simple but sturdy one-bedroom tent suitable for a couple for £100, while a big four-bedroom tent with windows, high ceilings and a sewn-in groundsheet to protect you from bugs and rain will set you back around £500. Many modern tents also come with fitted carpets for added insulation and comfort.

Yurts and tipis

Yurts, which are circular dwelling spaces with a domed roof, originated from Central Asia and have been around for centuries. Unlike conventional camping tents, yurts tend to have solid wooden floors, and you sleep in comfortable raised beds rather than on the ground. Yurt holiday operators can be found in numerous picturesque areas of the country, from the Cotswolds to Cornwall and the Scilly Isles. There are even luxury yurts with four-poster beds and roll-top baths, but yurt sites do not have electricity, and cooking is usually done on a wood-burning stove. The emphasis is on sustainable living, rather than luxury, but in recent years yurts have become the cool way to camp.

Feather Down Farms

Feather Down Farms have been causing quite a stir in the luxury camping market in the past couple of years, offering the opportunity to sample rustic life on a real working farm. Accommodation consists of spacious tents with decking floors, canvas walls and wood-fired ovens on which to cook. You can gather your own eggs for breakfast and participate in the working life of the farm. At present there are 24 farm locations around the UK, with more planned to open.

The National Trust

The National Trust promotes camping at a handful of its most beautiful and historic locations. Perhaps the most stunning of all is Wasdale in the Lake District, which scooped the accolade of Britain's Favourite View, as voted for by ITV viewers. If you don't fancy a tent, you can book into an on-site pod – a wooden dome with insulated, wool-lined walls and carpets.

Top British holiday websites

- www.goodbeachguide.co.uk
- www.beach-huts.com
- www.scoobycampers.com
- www.havenholidays.co.uk
- www.butlins.co.uk
- www.featherdown.co.uk
- www.yurt-holidays.co.uk
- www.campingandcaravanningclub.co.uk
- www.bigfreeguide.com

Holiday for less

House swapping

House swapping has become the fashionable way to holiday during the recession, particularly among the middle classes. Living in a real home offers a fantastic opportunity to sample authentic life in a different country, as well as saving a small fortune on accommodation costs. The UK's biggest home-swap agency, Home Link, has been organising house swaps since the 1950s. It organises over 13,000 swaps each year in over 65 different countries and has offices in 20 different countries, so swappers can be assured of a high level of experienced support.

As well as saving on accommodation costs, house swapping may also afford you the opportunity to travel further afield, or for a longer period of time. It is perfectly possible to organise a month's stay in Australia or America for little more than the cost of the flights. And, contrary to popular opinion, you do not need to live in a well-known town or city to appeal to international swappers. Indeed, many experienced house swappers are seasoned travellers who have already visited the popular tourist sights and are keen to explore less well-known areas of the country.

How to organise a house swap

There are several house-swap agencies. Most will charge a registration fee, which includes a listing of your home. The following is a step-by-step guide to organising a successful house swap.

1. *Post an ad*. Write a description of your home, including details such as how many bedrooms and bathrooms you have, whether you have a garden, any features that make your home distinctive, and what mod-cons are included (e.g. dishwasher, satellite TV, DVD player, and so on). Also state whether the swapper will have use of your car. Write a description of your neighbourhood too, detailing access to public transport, and any nearby historic sites and areas of natural beauty. Make your ad appealing, but

be honest and include as many photos as possible of your home and area.

2. *Be clear about your requirements.* Specify if you are happy for children and/or pets to stay in your home, what facilities are available and if you have any pets yourself. State clearly if any relatives are living in the property or are likely to visit, and if you have any regular domestic services, such as a cleaning lady or dog-walker.

3. *Communicate.* When you have found a fellow house swapper, it's a good idea to exchange e-mails and chat on the phone so that you can ask each other questions.

4. *Check the contract.* Agencies have standard contracts that should include a guarantee that swappers will pay for any damage. You should inform your home insurer of the swap, and also your motor insurer if use of a car is included in the arrangement.

Top home exchange agencies

- Home Link: www.homelink.org.uk
- Homebase Hols: www.homebase-hols.com
- Home Exchange: www.homeexchange.com
- Swap My City Pad: www.swapmycitypad.com

Retreats

A few days at a retreat is the perfect and affordable antidote to the stress of looking after children over the six-week summer break. Retreat centres are essentially quiet houses. Many are located in beautiful settings, and they offer comfortable accommodation and excellent home-cooked food that would not shame a country hotel, but at a fraction of the cost. Some centres may also offer bursaries to those unable to meet the full cost of a stay. The Retreat Associations website, www.retreats.org.uk lists centres across the UK.

Free bed

If you're a student, young single or couple, you may want to consider joining the couchsurfing community, which enables you to take up the offer of free accommodation around the world. The site www.couch surfing.org connects travellers with locals in 230 different countries. You'll need to create a profile on the site to get started, and the site also recommends linking up with other couchsurfing travellers and building up references before you begin to look for hosts.

Spring clean your cupboards

Use the last few days of August to de-clutter your cupboards and make some extra cash by recycling unwanted mobile phones, books and furniture, in time for the new school year in September.

- Mobile phones – a number of companies will pay for you to recycle an old mobile phone. You could earn up to £150 for a phone in decent working condition. Log on to a couple of the mobile phone comparison sites to see how much you could get for your old mobile – for example, www.comparemymobile.com, www.sellmymobile.com and www.mobilephonerecycling.co.uk.

- Books – sell unwanted books on Amazon or eBay or send in paperbacks to www.greenmetropolis.com. You'll get £3 for every book sold, and a donation is also made to the Woodland Trust.

- Furniture – offload unwanted furniture for free at www.gumtree.co.uk.

Restore last year's school uniforms

It must be a slightly depressing sight for your children to see shops stocking up with back to school gear well before the summer holidays have even started! Instead of rushing out to buy new uniforms and sports kit for the new school term, revive ink-stained shirts, sport socks and faded sweatshirts using some old-fashioned home laundry tricks.

Remove ink stains and sweat patches
Soak ink-stained shirts in milk overnight and launder as usual the next day. To remove sweat patches from white shirts crush an aspirin in a bowl of warm water and soak the shirts for a couple of hours, then launder as usual. The shirts will be sparkling clean, thanks to the effervescent effect of the aspirin.

Remove grease
To remove grease marks from synthetic fabrics such as polyester, sprinkle some talcum powder directly on to the stain and rub it in with your fingers. Leave for 24 hours, and then gently brush the stain away. Repeat this as necessary until the mark has been removed completely.

Brighten up colours
If your old winter clothes are looking a little tired and faded revive their colour by adding 100ml white vinegar to your wash cycle. The clothes will come out looking bright and fresh.

Prevent lost buttons and runs in tights
Putting a drop of clear nail varnish on the thread of buttons on new school shirts will prevent the threads from fraying and the buttons from falling off. If you spot a run in fragile tights or stockings, dabbing a little nail varnish on to the end of the run will stop it from spreading further.

Use a paper clip as a zip pull
There's no need to throw away a jacket or schoolbag just because the zip pull is broken. Untwist a small paperclip enough to slip it through the hole and twist it closed again to zip up.

Combat smelly sports socks

Sports socks are often full of bacteria and fungi that don't always come out in the wash. Adding a cup of sugar-free mouthwash during the wash cycle will help get rid of any odour. Mouthwash can also be used to get rid of dandruff.

Loosen knots and tangles

Don't break your nails trying to untie knots and tangles from shoelaces. Sprinkle some talcum powder on to the laces (or any knotted cords) and the knots will pull apart more easily. Talcum powder also helps untangle chain necklaces.

Buy half-price school shoes

Check out your nearest Clarks outlet store. As in the high street stores the fitters are fully trained, but the shoes usually cost around half the price of the regular retail price.

Protect new shoes from scuffs

The backs and toes of leather shoes take the brunt of surface wear and tear. Paint a little clear nail varnish over the toes and back seams of new shoes to increase their longevity.

9 September

September marks the end of the long summer holidays and a return to the routine of school and work. Some people regard September as a 'second New Year' and a time for making fresh starts. If you've been following the *Perfect Money Saving* programme since the beginning of the year, now is a good time to reflect on the savings you have made so far and perhaps considering if there are any further improvements you could make. For example, now that the children are back at school could you save money by cooking double quantities of family meals and freezing them? Perhaps you could halve your weekly grocery bill by shopping at a discount supermarket?

September is also a good month to review your utility suppliers to check that you are getting the best deals on your gas, electricity, home phone and broadband. New regulations mean that gas and electricity suppliers have to provide you with a clear annual statement showing how much energy you have consumed and, more importantly, which tariff you are currently on. A new Ofcom ruling, introduced in the summer of 2010, means that it is also much cheaper to change your home phone provider.

With just four months to go until Christmas, September is a good month to look at ways of bringing in some extra cash. If you have a son or daughter who is heading off to university, you could earn up to £4,250 a year tax free by letting the spare room in your home. If the idea of having a lodger doesn't appeal but you are lucky enough to have a driveway that you do not use, you could earn up to £200 a week letting it out as a parking space – long-term parking spaces close to busy commuter stations are always in demand. Another way of earning a few extra pounds is to sell cosmetics for a company such as Avon or the Body Shop. Most new consultants manage to make at least £50 a week hosting 'product parties', and surplus stock can be used as Christmas presents.

Or, if you are heading off to university next month, open a student bank account now so that it is up and running before you arrive at campus. Typically, new students simply opt for an account at their parents' bank, but this may not represent the best value, and nor will opting for an account just for the free music or shopping vouchers. A generous interest-free overdraft and free railcard will pay better financial dividends in the long run, so use a comparison site to compare the available accounts.

Food shopping

Foods in season this month

Cucumbers, damsons, figs, onions, oysters and plums.

Choosing figs: Figs do not ripen after picking, so look for soft fruits with a rich colour and unbroken skins. The ripest may be covered in a slight fuzz. Avoid figs with a sour smell – these fruits are overripe and past their best.

Storing oysters: Kept in an open container covered with wet kitchen towels, unopened oysters should keep for two to three days, but throw away any that open during this time. Shucked oysters can be refrigerated for up to four days if kept in a sealed container, and they are also suitable for freezing.

Stop frozen bread from getting soggy

If you prepare homemade lunch boxes for your kids, chances are you'll buy bread in bulk and freeze several loaves at a time. To prevent the bread from going soggy as it defrosts, place a paper towel around the loaf before you put it in the freezer. The towel will absorb moisture as the bread thaws.

Save on utility bills

Gas and electricity

In a bid to simplify bills, utility companies now have to provide their customers with an annual statement showing how much gas or electricity they consume in a year, and how much they can expect to pay the following year. They also have to state clearly which tariff your bills are currently based on. This information is vital because it is impossible to compare suppliers without knowing your tariff, and, according to Ofcom, in July 2010 there were 559 different active tariffs. Use a price comparison site to see if you could save money by switching suppliers.

Home phone and broadband

In June 2010 the regulator Ofcom announced that the main telephone landline providers BT, TalkTalk and Virgin Media had agreed to lower their charges when customers opted out of their landline phone or broadband contracts before the contracts expired, so it is now possible to shop around for the best broadband and phone line suppliers in the same way as you do for gas and electricity suppliers. The savings can be significant. For example, before June 2010 BT used to charge customers who wanted to leave its Weekend package before the end of their contract an exit fee of £11.54 a month. However, since Ofcom stepped in it has reduced the fee to just £2.

As with energy suppliers, phone providers offer a bewildering array of different call tariffs and broadband packages, so it pags to shop around.

Top websites for switching suppliers

To help navigate the minefield and find the best package for you, check out a couple of the following switching sites:

- www.homephonechoices.co.uk
- www.simplifydigital.co.uk
- www.moneysupermarket.com
- www.uswitch.com

Money-makers

With Christmas just around the corner, September is a good month to make some extra cash.

Let out your spare room or garage

You can earn up to £4,250 a year (or £81 a week) tax free by letting out a spare room in your house. If you don't want a full-time lodger, you could let a room from Monday to Friday to a local professional. The specialist websites www.spareroom.co.uk and www.easyroommate. co.uk are good places to advertise a spare room, as is Gumtree.

If you live in close to a busy town centre or railway station and have a driveway or garage that you do not use, you could earn around £10,000 a year by renting it out (depending on the location and demand for such spaces). The two main websites that offer this service are www.parkatmyhouse.co.uk and www.parklet.co.uk, both of which allow you to place an ad for free; they reckon that you can earn between £100 and £200 a week.

If you live in an urban area where parking space is at a premium and are fortunate enough to have a front garden, consider digging up the lawn and connecting the area into a parking space. It will cost between £10,000 and £20,000 to get paving slabs laid, although you may also need to obtain planning permission from your local council, but surveys show that it could add as much as an extra £50,000 to the value of an expensive urban property.

Become a cosmetics rep

A fun way of earning some extra cash in time for Christmas and building up a stash of presents, is to become a cosmetics representative. Representatives earn money by selling make-up and skincare products at product parties and classes, or through catalogues and websites. To set yourself up as a representative you will have to purchase a starter kit containing a variety of beauty products to sell, learn how to demonstrate the company's products and build up a client base. It is important to remember that you will have to invest in the company by buying products at the outset, and you will make money only if the value of your sales exceeds your initial outlay.

As with any sales job, you are most likely to be successful if you genuinely believe in the products and if you get to know your customers. Most companies reckon you can make £50–60 at a product party, so if you can manage to host one a week in the three-month run up to Christmas you could make over £700 in total. More ambitious representatives build bigger earnings by recruiting other representatives to sell for them. In this sense, the industry works a bit like a pyramid (though it should not be confused with the pyramid-selling scam). Top area sales directors can turnover more than £150,000 and enjoy free holidays to exotic destinations, gala dinners and even company cars.

Avon

The Avon lady was an iconic image of the 1970s. However, the company has modernised its brand and now sports a range of men's skincare products as well as a children's range. There is a growing number of male representatives, and Avon is also marketing itself as a career route for new graduates. The company, which was founded by an American door-to-door bookseller in 1886, now has sales representatives in 100 countries. It claims that a third of British women use Avon products, and it sells one lipstick every three seconds in one of the 100 countries in which the company retails.

As an Avon representative you can make £1 for every £4 of products you sell.

Body Shop

Body Shop consultants earn commission by hosting Body Shop parties in their own homes. You will have to purchase a 'bag for life' pamper kit, which contains a range of products, and catalogues that you can carry with you to drum up interest when you go to work, do the school run or go to the gym. An area manager provides training in demonstrating and selling the products. As a consultant you are required to host a minimum of four parties in four weeks, but there are no minimum sales levels you must achieve, and consultants earn 25 per cent commission.

An initial pamper kit costs £40, and the Body Shop reckons that an average consultant makes approximately £50 at each party.

Vie at Home

Vie at Home is a British direct-selling company that was relaunched in 2009, following a management buy-out from the Virgin Group. In addition to cosmetics, it also sells its own range of jewellery and home-wares. Like Body Shop consultants, Vie at Home consultants make their money by hosting special themed product parties, which can include pampering parties, makeover parties, hen night parties, aromatherapy parties, homeware parties, or even simple one-to-one consultations. New consultants are given training in how to sell Vie's products and how to carry out makeovers and facials.

The starter kit costs £44.50 for over £395 worth of products. You should be able to earn back your initial outlay at your first party and be well on the way to making some profit.

Mary Kay

Mary Kay is an upmarket cosmetics brand that was founded in the USA in the early 1960s, and it entered the UK market in 2004. As with

Avon, Mary Kay consultants sell direct to friends, family, neighbours and work colleagues, and they earn commission in the form of a 40 per cent discount off the product price. However, the most successful Mary Kay consultants earn money by recruiting other consultants to sell on their behalf.

Indeed, the route to becoming a Mary Kay consultant is by being introduced through another consultant. You will then need to purchase a starter pack (currently £185 for £400 worth of products) and undergo training. Most product selling and networking is done at Mary Kay 'classes' which are set up by the consultant or other women they know. Classes are similar to product parties, but instead of the consultant giving clients a makeover, customers are taught how to give themselves a facial, apply make-up and use the products themselves.

The initial start-up cost for Mary Kay consultants is high compared with some other cosmetic brands, but the company offers an excellent buy-back guarantee scheme whereby if you decide to opt out of the job, the company will buy back 90 per cent of any unused products you have already paid for.

Student finances

If you're off to university next month, open a student bank account now and work out your budget. Add up how much income you are expecting from loans, grants, parental contributions and part-time jobs, and then deduct expenses for accommodation, food, travel, books and entertainment.

Since the introduction of tuition fees, more students are adopting the American route of working their way through college, and most university campuses offer part-time job opportunities in libraries, shops and bars. If you have specialist skills, you might be able to earn extra cash giving music or foreign language lessons or by designing websites. In October 2010 the minimum hourly wage was £5.93, so if you can get 20 hours of work each week during term time, your rent and food bills should be covered.

Student bank accounts

Most banks will allow students to open a bank account if they have a UCAS offer, so it's possible to open an account before you arrive at university. All banks will try to bribe you with freebies and vouchers, but by far the most useful feature of a student bank account is an interest-free overdraft. In 2010 Halifax and the Bank of Scotland were offering interest-free overdrafts of up to £3,000, and Barclays was offering up to £2,000. The Royal Bank of Scotland offers an interest-free overdraft up to £2,750, plus a free railcard for 16- to 25-year-olds for three years (worth £65 a year) to Scottish students or those studying at a Scottish university.

Whichever bank you choose, make sure you agree on overdraft limit in advance and do not exceed it. Fees for unauthorised overdrafts can be as high as 30 per cent, plus extra charges on top. The comparison sites www.moneysupermarket.com and www.moneyfacts.co.uk can help identify the best account for your needs.

Student savings

- *Get free theatre tickets.* If you are under 26 you can get free theatre tickets at more than 200 venues across England as part of an Arts Council Scheme. Log on to www.anightless ordinary.org and type in your postcode to find which theatres near you are taking part.

- *Download free music.* The free internet jukebox Spotify (www.spotify.com) allows you to download software and access millions of songs and music tracks from Brahms to the Beatles.

- *Get a cut-price iPod or Mac.* If you're an Apple fan, you could bag a bargain buying a refurbished iPod or iBook from Apple's online store at www.store.apple.com/uk. Refurbished items are covered by a one-year guarantee. Apple also regularly offers discounts to students in possession of a valid NUS card.

10 October

Autumn has been called the season of mists and mellow fruitfulness, but as the nights draw in and the clocks go back, we also rack up our heating and lighting bills. Energy Saving Week is held in October, so this month look at ways of reducing your heating and lighting bills.

The Energy Saving Trust has calculated that the average household could save up to £340 on its gas and electricity bills by making their home more energy efficient. Local councils and energy companies are sitting on oodles of cash – in the form of unclaimed grants and benefits that are available to homeowners to install cavity wall and loft insulation. As we saw in the May chapter, if you want to sell your home you have to provide an energy efficiency graph for your property, and in July 2010 the government announced details of plans to levy an extra 0.5 per cent stamp duty on buyers purchasing properties that fall into the lowest energy efficiency band. So, if you are selling a home worth £500,000 and it has a poor energy efficiency rating, your buyer could negotiate an extra £2,500 off their final offer to cover the extra stamp duty bill.

But even if you are not planning to move, you can save hundreds of pounds on your gas and electricity bills by insulating the walls and lofts. You can obtain a personalised report on the energy efficiency of your home, and identify where you can make energy savings, on the Energy Saving Trust's website at www.energysaving trust.org.uk.

Halloween falls around the October half-term. Most children love dressing up, and witches' dresses and ghost outfits can be created cheaply and easily from black bin liners and old white sheets. Pumpkins, quintessential to Halloween, double up as jack-o'-lanterns and the main ingredient in delicious homemade soups and pies. You can pick up a large pumpkin for about £1 at most supermarkets.

The October half-term is also a good time to start making Christmas cards, decorations and presents, and to plan a 'booze cruise' across the channel to stock up on good-value wines and foods to fill Christmas hampers.

Food shopping

Foods in season this month

Apples, figs, elderberries, pumpkin and watercress.

Storing apples: Apples keep for much longer than most fruits, and fruit in good condition can be stored for up to a month and sometimes longer. To retain the flavour, keep apples cool – they will last much longer in a plastic bag placed in the fridge than they will in the fruit bowl.

Storing watercress: Watercress is quick to wilt and perish. It is best kept in the fridge, with the stems in a glass of water, covered with a plastic bag.

Go foraging

Autumn is a great time to go foraging. Hedgerow berries, chestnuts, damsons, sloes, apples, pears and rosehip grow in abundance in many areas and can be used to make delicious jams, pies and crumbles. Richard Mabey's book *Food for Free* is an excellent guide.

Plan a booze cruise

You can save over 50 per cent on a case of wine at a French hypermarket. Because the excise duties are much lower in France than the UK, you're also likely to save at least 30 per cent on spirits, whisky and cognac. Cheeses, pâtés, olive oils, cold meats and chocolates are also likely to be good value. Save on channel-crossing fares by booking a midweek trip at an off-peak time.

Visit www.ferryonline.co.uk for price comparisons and special offers for the main ferry operators and www.day-tripper.net for general information on ferries, and price guides on food bargains abroad.

Make your home more energy efficient

Install good insulation

Good home insulation will save you money throughout the year. The Home Heat Helpline estimates that having cavity wall and loft insulation installed can cut your winter heating bills by 15 per cent, while fitting an insulating jacket on your hot water tank will save a further £30 each year.

Most energy companies offer grants of up to 50 per cent to almost any homeowner wishing to install insulation, and everyone over the age of 70 is entitled to free insulation from their energy company. Families on low incomes and people with disabilities or long-term health conditions may also qualify.

Switch off appliances

Get into the habit of switching off appliances such as kettles, TVs, computers and hi-fi systems at the power button or plug when you have finished using them. Appliances left on standby can use as much as three-quarters of the energy they use when they are switched on.

Given that the average home has at least eight appliances on standby, you could could save £32 on an average annual electricity bill by switching off at the socket.

Get a smart meter

By 2020 every home in Britain will have to be fitted with a smart meter, which will send real-time information on how much gas and electricity you are using direct to your utility company. Many energy companies are already offering their customers a trial meter, so take up the offer and monitor how much energy you consume.

Turn down the thermostat

Walking around the house in a T-shirt and shorts in the middle of winter is financial madness as well as environmentally unethical. Turning down the thermostat by just one degree can cut your heating bills by 10 per cent giving a typical saving of £65 a year. Make sure you switch off radiators in rooms that are not being used and keep internal doors shut.

Check for draughty windows and doors that may be letting heat escape. Close curtains at dusk, tucking them behind the radiator – curtains that drape over radiators and heaters waste heat by allowing heat to fly out of the window.

Save energy in the kitchen

Don't overfill the kettle
Boiling a full kettle of water to make a single cup of tea can cost you an extra £30 in electricity a year, so only boil the amount of water you need.

Put lids on pans
Most of us also waste a criminal amount of heat when we are cooking. If you put lids on pans when you are boiling, steaming or frying foods you will reduce cooking times (and, in turn, your energy bills) by a whopping 75 per cent. To boil pasta, rice or vegetables, place them in

a pan with cold water, put the lid on, bring the water to a rolling boil, give the contents a quick stir, then simply replace the lid and switch off the heat. The foods will cook in steam in exactly the same amount of time as if you'd left them to simmer. You'll also be surprised how much fresher and more distinctive they taste. If you cook this way every day for 20 minutes, it could save you over 7,000 hours of heat a year.

Defrost the fridge and freezer

Defrosting your fridge and freezer regularly will help them to run more efficiently and economically, so give your appliances a quick service before stocking up for Christmas.

Autumn garden maintenance

Scoop up garden leaves

Sweeping up autumn leaves from the lawn can be a back-breaking chore. Instead of constantly lifting piles of leaves on to a wheelbarrow or into a bag, sweep them all on to an old bedsheet laid on the ground, then simply gather up the four corners of the sheet, drag it to the leaf pile or compost heap, and empty the leaves out.

Protect gardening tools

To protect your gardening tools over the winter, fill a large bucket with builder's sand and a litre of clean motor oil. Plunge spades, hoes, rakes and other tools into the mixture several times to clean and lubricate them, before storing them away until spring. Storing tools in a bucket of sand will prevent them from rusting.

Half-term treats

Half-term is the perfect time to treat the family by taking advantage of offers of cheap eats and discounted entertainment.

Bargain theatre tickets

If you want to to take in a specific show this half-term, log on to www.theatremonkey.co.uk. Theatremonkey collates current promotions from newspapers and other sources.

Join the club

If you eat regularly at popular chains such as Giraffe, La Tasca or Wagamama you can save a considerable amount of money by joining the restaurants' own clubs. Most are free to join, and some, such as the tapas chain La Tasca, will give you a voucher on joining.

Cinema savings

In 2010 mobile phone company Orange was offering two-for-one cinema tickets to its customers every Wednesday, and it also teamed up with Pizza Express to offer two-for-one pizza deals. Many cinemas, including Vue, also offer significantly reduced price tickets for children on Saturday and Sunday mornings, and admit accompanying adults for free.

Make Christmas cards

There are hundreds of free websites from which you can send an e-card, but this may strike you as a little too cheap, and receiving an e-card can be rather annoying. After all, we all like to embellish our living rooms and mantelpieces with cards at Christmas. With a little creative inspiration – and a stack of coloured papers, cards, glitter, sequins, ribbons, photos and cuttings from magazines and flyers you can produce some impressive homemade creations. If you or your children come up with a particularly original design, do enter it for a Christmas card competition. For futher inspiration, take a look at. www.making-greeting-cards.com, www.allcrafts.net/cards and www.make-stuff.com.

11 November

Last month we looked at slashing heating and electricity bills over the autumn and winter months. As the nights really start to draw in it is also a good idea to check up on home security. If you or the other members of your family usually don't return home from school or work before it gets dark, programme an automatic timer to switch on a couple of lights at dusk so that your home does not look unoccupied.

Insurance companies say they receive more claims for burglaries after Bonfire Night, 5 November, than at any other time during the year. Loud noises from firework displays and large numbers of unattended properties mean thefts and break-ins are more likely to go unnoticed. If you are letting off fireworks in your own garden, close all windows and doors to avoid accidental damage, and keep your pets indoors.

Shops begin filling in earnest with Christmas stock by mid-November, and the rush is on to get the Christmas shopping and food preparations done. If you've been following the advice in this book so far you'll already have a stash of homemade hampers and gifts as well as stocking fillers and cheap presents that you picked up in the July sales, so this year's Christmas bill shouldn't break the bank. If you are super-organised your freezer may also already be stocked with sausage rolls, quiches, bread sauce, bacon-wrapped sausages and pastry for mince pies. If it's not, now is the time to get cracking.

With everyone's thoughts focused on Christmas, November can be a good month to pick up a bargain investment property. Property repossessions have soared in the past couple of years as the number of homeowners defaulting on their mortgages has increased. Lenders who repossess a property have a legal obligation to obtain the best price they can for the home, but they are also keen to sell quickly, and you could save up to 30 per cent on the market price in the run up to Christmas. Buying a repossessed property carries certain risks, of course, which is why they tend to appeal more to investment buyers than residential ones.

An unexpected windfall is welcome at any time of the year, but especially Christmas. It is estimated that there is about £15 billion sitting in dormant accounts and forgotten investments. So if you think you may have a few quid stashed away in a children's bank account that you opened decades ago, check the Unclaimed Assets Register. It may prove to be your best Christmas present yet!

Food shopping

Foods in season this month

Beetroot, chestnuts, cranberries, goose and parsnips.

Choosing chestnuts: Look for nuts that have smooth, shiny shells. Chestnuts shrivel after picking, so choose nuts that feel heavy for their size, and give them a squeeze to check that the nut inside has not dried out.

Choosing and storing beetroot: Smaller bulbs are more tender, and you should pick ones with smooth, undamaged surfaces. Store beetroot in an unsealed plastic bag in the fridge, with the leaves cut off.

Choosing parsnips: Look for parsnips that are firm, dry and relatively small – larger parsnips are more likely to have tough, woody cores.

Faster baked potatoes

Jacket potatoes are the perfect food for a Bonfire Night celebration indoors. Stick four wooden toothpicks into one side of each potato to create a set of four 'legs', before baking them in the microwave. The potatoes will cook much faster and more evenly because the microwave will reach the bottom and sides of the potato as well as the top.

Christmas preparations

Supermarket canapés, bacon-wrapped sausages, bread sauces, brandy butter and mince pies cost four times as much as they would to make at home, and you will save a great deal of money by making your own party foods and Christmas lunch trimmings. Pastry freezes particularly well, so November is a good month to start shopping for Christmas ingredients and making all the extras.

Buy a repossessed property

Repossessed properties tend to be sold by estate agents in the first instance, and then by auction if they remain unsold. If you go to auction to buy a repossessed property, you should be aware that it has probably been on the market for several months without attracting a buyer. Bear in mind that mortgage lenders use repossession as a last resort, so most homeowners who do find themselves in financial hardship try to sell their home themselves first.

Tips for buying a repossessed property

- *Do your research.* If you are buying a property to let, research rental rates and rental potential in your area. University towns and cities generally have a high demand for rental property, but be aware that if you let your property out to undergraduate students, there may be long periods during the summer holidays in which the house is unoccupied.

- *Familiarise yourself with the process.* Obtain auction catalogues, study conditions of sale on lots, property deeds and leases, and attend a couple of auctions as a viewer, to get a feel for how the procedure works.

- *Assess the condition of the property.* Most repossessed properties will require work, so view the property with a builder if you can and ask for quotes for making any repairs that may need to be carried out.

- *Get a survey.* If you win the bid at auction you are obliged to hand over the deposit and proceed with the sale there and then, so get a survey carried out first. You will lose the money you spend on it if you don't win the bid, but buying any property without a survey is madness.

- *Arrange your mortgage.* If you win the bid you will have to proceed with the sale, so you *must* have your mortgage arranged in advance and the deposit ready.

- *Set your limit and stick to it.* Having done your market research and obtained a survey and quotes for repairs, decide on the maximum price you are prepared to pay for the property and stick to it.

- *Familiarise yourself with tax liabilities.* You pay tax on rental income but can deduct mortgage interest. You can also claim income tax relief on repairs and redecoration (but not capital home improvements). Finally, if the property is not your main residence you will have to pay capital gains tax (CGT) on any profit you make above the CGT threshold when you sell.

Unclaimed assets

Do you have a children's savings account you opened back in the days when HBSC was still known as Midland Bank? Or perhaps you started an investment fund and forgot about it? The Unclaimed Assets Register estimates that there is over £15 billion in dormant accounts sitting in Britain's financial coffers. In July 2010 the government announced that it would be using money from dormant accounts to fund its 'Big Society' project, so if you think you may have Premium Bond prizes, savings or investments that you've forgotten about, grab them now.

Top unclaimed asset finders

- Unclaimed Assets Register: www.uar.co.uk
- My Lost Account: www.mylostaccount.org.uk
- National Savings & Investments: www.nsandi.com
- Pensions Tracing Service www.pensionsadvisoryservice.org.uk
- Pensions Scheme Registry: www.thepensionsregulator.gov.uk

12 December

If you've been following the money-saving programme since the beginning of the year you should be thousands of pounds better off than you were this time last Christmas. You may also have spread the cost of Christmas by picking up presents during sales and offer periods through the year; building up a stash of homemade gifts, stocking fillers, cards, gift wraps and hampers; and stocking your freezer with cheap food before the seasonal rush. If so, congratulations – this Christmas should be a money-saving breeze.

If you've just dipped into the book at this point, don't panic. You can still cut the cost of Christmas significantly by shopping at discount and cashback sites, making your own decorations, and – if you are hosting a large family Christmas lunch – asking each guest to bring a ready-cooked dish. You can also rustle up some free presents by gifting your time and talents or by picking up tickets to your family's or friends' favourite BBC shows. If you don't mind working, you can earn double rates childminding, pet-sitting, driving or waitressing on New Year's Eve.

Food shopping

When it comes to food shopping, less really is more. There are so many different components to a traditional Christmas lunch that you don't need more than a couple of morsels of any one item for each plate. Before filling up your trolley with all the trimmings, think about whether your family actually likes Brussels sprouts, cranberry sauce, brandy butter, or Stilton – according to the website www.lovefoodhatewaste.com, the average family wastes one-third of all the food it buys at Christmas. It is also worth remembering that most corner shops open on Boxing Day, so nobody is going to starve if you do happen is run out of any essential staples.

Share the cost and effort of Christmas cooking

By far the cheapest and most stress-free way of putting together a full-blown Christmas lunch is to ask each guest to contribute an item. It is probably easiest if the host cooks and provides the turkey and gravy. However, other guests can rustle up roast potatoes, vegetables, trimmings, a Christmas pudding and mince pies the night before, and zap them in the oven when they arrive. Most kitchens resemble Turkish baths on Christmas morning, so conserve heat by switching off the hob and allowing vegetables to steam in lid-covered pans, as explained in the October chapter.

The turkey

Most of us love a cold turkey sandwich, risotto or curry on Boxing Day but tire of it soon after that, so buy the correct sized bird for the number of diners. As a general guide, you need a pound of poultry for each person, so if you are catering for under ten people work on the basis that a 6lb bird will be sufficient for six people, and an 8lb bird will be enough for eight people. The ratios vary slightly when you get into double figures: an 18lb bird, for example, should comfortably feed twenty people. If you are a small family of four, a turkey crown may be better value than a small whole bird. Frozen turkeys are cheaper than fresh ones, so look out for offers at the beginning of the month.

Keep leftover cake fresh

To keep leftover Christmas cake fresher for longer, put a couple of sugar cubes into an airtight container with the cake. Adding a few sugar lumps to a food storage container can also prevent cheese from going mouldy.

> ## Juicy roast ham
>
> To make a succulent and juicy ham, pour a can of cola over the joint before marinating and baking it in the normal way.

Stock up on drinks

Christmas and New Year is the season for plenty of wine and bubbly. Get better quality drinks for less by careful shopping at the supermarket or by buying in bulk.

Try supermarket own-brand wines

Just as popular branded foods often cost more but taste the same as supermarket own brands, supermarket wines are often as good as (and frequently judged superior to) more famous labels but come at a fraction of the price. At the 2010 International Wine Challenge awards, British supermarkets scooped a total of 257 medals for their own-brand wines, and the majority were priced under £10. In 2009 Asda's Portuguese rosé (£2.98) beat several wines costing up to £40 a bottle at the Decanter World Wine Awards.

Supermarket wines are often made by the same winemakers and at the same wineries as more famous brands. For example, Sainsbury's Taste the Difference Chilean Sauvignon Blanc is made by exactly the same winemaker using grapes from the same region (and at the same winery) as the well-regarded Erazuriz Sauvignon Blanc. Marks & Spencer's Ayala Champagne is made by the same company that produces Bollinger. Use a website such as www.quaffersoffers.co.uk to search for the best current wine offers at supermarkets and specialist wine merchants.

Be wary of half-price bin-ends

Supermarkets often heavily market half-price bin-end wines that are reduced from, say, £7.99 to £3.99, especially at Christmas. However, such promotions have come in for some criticism from wine experts, who claim that the wines are 'marked up to be marked down' so that the 'half-price' ticket in fact reflects the wine's true price. It is also worth remembering that you pay £1 in UK tax for every bottle of wine you buy, regardless of its quality. When you factor in the cost of producing and shipping the wine, plus the cost of the bottle itself, a mid-priced wine, costing £5–6, may represent better overall value than a bargain-priced one costing £3.99.

Warehouse deals

Wine warehouses such as Majestic Wines often offer some great deals, especially on cases of 12 bottles. They will often allow you to sample wines before you buy, and mix and match bottles of the same price to make up a case. If you choose carefully, you can save at least 20 per cent on wines and spirits at a warehouse.

Wine clubs

Wine clubs such as the *Sunday Times* wine club, as well as specialist wine retailers such as Laithwaites, offer great introductory offers on cases of 12 bottles. This is a good way of sampling high-quality wines at reasonable prices. Cases are often made up of two lots of six different bottles, so it may be worth clubbing together with a friend to split the cost of a case.

Top discount drink websites

- www.sundaytimeswineclub.co.uk
- www.laithwaites.co.uk
- www.virginwines.com
- www.majestic.co.uk

Decorating your home

The Christmas tree

An artificial tree costs much less than a real one, saves hoovering up pine needles and, of course, can be used again year after year. Decorate your tree using lights with LED bulbs, which use 90 per cent less electricity than conventional incandescent bulbs; they can be found in most DIY shops or online at www.lights4fun.co.uk.

Homemade decorations

- Wrap chocolates, bite-sized biscuits or small matchboxes in different coloured shiny foil and hang them from the tree with gold thread.

- Gather pine cones, leave them to dry on the radiator for a few days and decorate them with gold and silver glitter or spray. They make stunning tree decorations and also look great scattered around the fireplace with some tangerines.

- Make your own Christmas crackers by wrapping long pieces of coloured foil or tissue paper around empty loo rolls and tying bits of gold thread at the ends to create a puffed gather. Fill your crackers with sweets, jokes, novelty items, party-poppers and, of course, the obligatory paper hats.

- Create a table centrepiece by sticking a candle on a sturdy piece of cardboard or wood covered in foil (or metallic spray). Surround it with ivy, silver- and gold-painted pine cones, and grapes dipped in beaten egg white and icing sugar.

- Make a Christmas wreath by unravelling an old wire coat hanger and bending it into a circle. Bind the wire with coloured ribbon and decorate it with holly, ivy and dried flowers.

- Make paper chains out of old magazines, coloured foil, brown paper and even newspapers sprayed with gold. To make a paper snowflake, cut out a circle of white paper, fold it in half and then into three equal sections. Use a sharp pair of scissors to cut out shapes along the fold and then open it up to admire the effects. You can decorate these with glitter or gold spray.

Inexpensive gifts

Presents don't have to cost the earth. With a bit of thought and effort there are plenty of ways you can give someone the perfect present without spending a lot – or even spending at all!

Low-cost presents

Stocking fillers

Now is the time to pull out all those free cosmetics samples, pens, notebooks, diaries, chocolates and other novelty items you've been collecting over the year to fill up stockings, homemade Christmas crackers and gift hampers (see p. 82 for some hamper ideas).

Top discount book sites

Books are classic Christmas presents, but don't assume that you'll find the best price on Amazon. Use a couple of the sites below to find the cheapest supplier for the title you want to purchase.

- www.books.co.uk

- www.bestbookprice.co.uk

- www.comparebookprices.co.uk

Profit from mistakes

So many items on eBay remain unsold because they have been spelled incorrectly in the listings that there is now a website, www.fatfingers.co.uk, dedicated to them. Even if you don't end up buying anything, you might discover some amusing anecdotes to entertain your Christmas guests.

Luxury treats and experience gifts

Spa days, cookery lessons, roller-blading sessions and motor racing days make lovely gifts. It is possible to save up to 70 per cent on the ticket price of such items through collective buying sites such as www.likebees.com and www.wowcher.co.uk.

Top discount cosmetics sites

Look at the following websites for discount perfumes, scents and half-price make-up:

- www.fragrancedirect.co.uk
- www.halfpriceperfumes.co.uk
- www.feelunique.co.uk

Leave it till the last minute

If you just can't bear the idea of starting your Christmas shopping in July, the next best thing is to leave it right until the last minute – if you're willing to take the risk, you'll find the best bargains after lunch on Christmas Eve.

No-cost presents

Gift your time or services

A few hours spent ironing, babysitting or dog-walking could be a much-valued gift to a busy mother rushed off her feet or an elderly relative. If you have music, language or sporting skills you could gift a course of ten piano lessons, or a crash course in Spanish, tennis or windsurfing.

Free tickets

Apply for free tickets to live BBC shows such as *Strictly Come Dancing*, *Mastermind* or *The Review Show* by logging on to www.bbc.co.uk/shows.

Quick Reference 1
The 'big' financial stuff

A core financial portfolio consists of savings, investments, mortgages, pensions and insurances. The bulk of this book has outlined numerous ways of saving money throughout the year and has suggested places in which to save it. In this section of the *Perfect Money Saving* programme we tackle the other big financial products.

Current accounts

We all need a current account in which to deposit our income and from which to pay bills and day-to-day living expenses. Current accounts also come with a variety of other incentives, such as overdrafts, interest paid on accounts in credit and free insurance products. It is important to choose the right current account for your needs. If you are regularly overdrawn, for example, choose an account that has a low rate on arranged overdrafts. On the other hand, if you always stay in credit you may benefit from an account that pays interest or offers free travel insurance.

The current account market is dominated by the 'big four' banks – Barclays, HSBC, Lloyds and the Royal Bank of Scotland – but in late 2010 a raft of new players – Metro, Virgin, Tesco and the Post Office, among others – indicated their intention to join the fray, bringing more competition to the current account market.

Switching current accounts

Many banks offer incentives, such as a £100 payment, to switch to their current account. Despite this, many of us are reluctant to change our current accounts. A survey by *Which?* found that three-quarters of customers had never changed their bank account. This may be because in the past changing a bank account was a long drawn-out, cumbersome affair that involved a lot of hassle and could take several weeks to complete.

New guidelines mean that it is much quicker and easier to change accounts than it used to be, however. Your old bank must pass on all information, including direct debits, standing orders and your credit history, to your new bank within three working days, and your new bank must open your account within ten working days of your application being approved. If you apply for a new account at a bank branch, you will be asked for two forms of identification and be asked to complete two forms: an application form and a transfer form. These should take no more than ten minutes to fill in.

When you are applying for a new account, make sure that the bank offers a free 'switcher' overdraft for any direct debits or standing orders that may be collected before the money is transferred to your new account.

Different types of current account

There are two types of current account – free accounts, on which you pay nothing, and fee accounts, for which you pay a monthly fee in return for a gamut of extras – such as travel or mobile phone insurance, higher interest or a premium service.

Overdrafts

Bank overdrafts are one of the most expensive ways of borrowing money, so the best advice is: don't go overdrawn. If you think you are likely to slip into the red for a short time, choose an account with a low rate of interest on overdrafts and agree an overdraft limit (to which you must stick). Fees for unauthorised overdrafts are exorbitant.

Mortgages

Unless you are lucky enough to own your home outright, your mortgage is likely to be your biggest financial outlay. The standard mortgage term is 25 years, over which you pay interest on the amount you have borrowed. Although mortgage rates are currently the lowest they have been for many years and mortgages are typically the cheapest form of debt on the market (mortgage rates are almost always lower than personal loan, overdraft and credit card rates), paying over the odds can cost you several thousands of pounds over a lifetime, so it is essential to keep your mortgage under review, ensuring you are getting the best value available.

Mortgage rates fluctuate according to the rate at which lenders can borrow money from the money markets and their own balance sheets. There are several types of mortgage rates: fixed, discounted, capped, tracker and the lender's standard variable rate. There are also different types of mortgage: capital repayment, interest-only and offset mortgages.

Fixed rates

Fixed-rate mortgages are a good bet if you want to know exactly how much you will be paying each month for a certain number of years. Rates can be fixed over one, two, five or sometimes ten years. Fixed rate mortgages provide certainty, but they usually also come with redemption penalties for redeeming the mortgage before the end of the term, so they are not a good choice if you are planning to move into a new home soon, or pay off your mortgage early.

Discounted and capped rates

As the term implies, discounted-rate mortgages offer a discount on the lender's standard variable rate. Like fixed-rate mortgages, discount mortgages usually run for a set number of years, and there will be redemption penalties for redeeming the mortgage before the end of the term. However, unlike fixed rates, the monthly payments on discounted rate mortgages can still go up or down depending on interest rate movements. So, if you take out a mortgage at a 2 per cent discount off the lender's standard variable rate of 4.5 per cent, you would pay 2.5 per cent. However, if interest rates rose by 0.5 per cent next month, you would pay 3 per cent. Capped rates work in the same way, except that the lender imposes a cap above which your mortgage rate cannot rise.

Tracker mortgages

Tracker mortgages mimic interest rate movements and so go up or down as the Bank of England base rate rises or falls. Lenders peg their tracker rates either at exactly the Bank of England's (BoE) current base rate or a slightly above or below the rate for a set period. At the end of 2010, the Bank of England base rate was 0.5 per cent, so if you had a tracker mortgage pegged at 1 per cent above the BoE rate, you would be paying 1.5 per cent interest on your mortgage. Tracker mortgages have been particularly good value in recent years as interest rates have fallen. Some canny borrowers who purchased tracker mortgages pegged at 0.75 or 1 per cent below the BoE rate have enjoyed interest-free mortgages for several months.

Standard variable rate

The standard variable rate (SVR) is the 'standard' rate at which banks and building societies lend to their mortgage customers. It is usually at least a couple of percentage points higher than the Bank of England's base rate, so if you are paying the SVR, check to see what other deals are available.

Offset/current account mortgages

Most people with a mortgage also have savings, no matter how paltry. An offset or current account mortgage basically acts as a savings account and mortgage rolled into one, and your savings offset your mortgage debt. If you had, for example, £200,000 outstanding on your home and savings of £20,000, with an offset mortgage the total debt on which you would pay interest is £180,000. By ploughing your savings into an offset mortgage you avoid paying tax on the interest, but you can still withdraw your savings when you need to.

As the name implies, current account mortgages (CAMs) combine your bank account with your mortgage. So if you have £2,000 in your current account and £100,000 outstanding on your mortgage, your statement will show your balance as £98,000 overdrawn.

CAMs offer the same services as ordinary current accounts. You can add savings and credit card debts on to the account and pay the same rate of interest on the lot. This type of mortgage may be suitable for self-employed people who may have large sums of money coming in at irregular intervals, and need to draw out money for tax bills and business purposes. It is not, however, recommended for the financially undisciplined.

Paying off your mortgage early

It makes sense to borrow heavily in times of high inflation because inflation reduces the value of your debt. However, in times of low inflation, the debt stays pretty much where it is, and you cannot rely on wage increases to reduce your debt. Inflation is currently relatively low and is likely to remain so for the foreseeable future, so if you do not have other debts, such as loans or credit cards, using the savings you have made from following the suggestions in this book to overpay your mortgage is probably the best investment you can make. The savings you will make as a result could enable you to fund two children through university and still have some left over. For example, if you made overpayments of £100 a month on a £100,000 mortgage taken out over a 25 year term, at a rate of 6 per cent, you would save just over £27,000 and knock six years off the term of your mortgage.

Check redemption penalties

Before you commit to making overpayments, check that that your lender will not impose a redemption penalty for paying off your mortgage early. Some lenders impose a minimum overpayment each month (this might be £50 or £100). If you pay less than this, the money will simply sit in the lender's coffers until the end of the financial year, rather than immediately reducing your debt – you will, in effect, have given them an interest-free loan.

If you have a special fixed or discounted rate deal, your lender is likely to impose redemption penalties for paying off your mortgage early. In such circumstances it is unwise to make overpayments as they will be eaten up by the penalties. Instead, put the extra money into a high-interest savings account. When your fixed or discounted rate deal expires and you remortgage, plough the savings into your new mortgage to reduce the overall debt.

To find out how much you can save by overpaying your mortgage or switching to a lower rate, use one of the many interactive calculators available on websites such as www.thisismoney.co.uk.

Savings

The first step to creating wealth is to build up a cash reserve that you can dip into for holidays, anniversaries, emergencies and at Christmas. With interest rates at an all-time low, you will not reap fantastic rewards on savings accounts. Indeed, barely a day goes by when we do not hear the refrain that savers are being 'robbed' by financial institutions. But low rates are not an excuse *not* to save. What is important is to get into the habit of saving regularly, so you always have money put aside for a rainy day. As Arkad, the eponymous 'rich man' in the enduring fable 'The Richest Man in Babylon', told his eager disciple: 'I found the road to wealth when I decided that a part of all I earned was mine to keep.' Indeed, saving means paying yourself first, so now that you have learned to slash your bills and outgoings, squirrel away the savings for yourself.

Individual Savings Accounts

The best place to invest your cash is in an Individual Savings Account (ISA), which allows your money to grow tax-free. There are two types of ISA – cash ISAs and stocks and shares ISAs – and it is a common misconception that an ISA is a savings or investment product in itself. In fact, an ISA is simply a wrapper than allows your money to grow tax free. But because the money you put into an ISA grows tax free, the government imposes limits on the amount you can put into one each year. For the tax year 2010–11 each person over the age of 18 was given an ISA allowance of £10,200, of which up to £5,100 of can be held in cash, with the remaining allowance invested in stocks and shares. Alternatively, you can invest your entire ISA allowance in stocks and shares alone. One of the best cash ISAs on the market at the end of 2010 was the Cheltenham & Gloucester, which paid 2.7 per cent interest.

National Savings and Investments

National Savings and Investments (NS&I) was set up in 1861 as the Post Office Savings Bank as a secure place in which the public could save their money. It remains true to those principles today, and offers a range of cash savings products such as investment accounts, fixed-term bonds, children's accounts and, of course, Premium Bonds. All products are tax free and guaranteed by the Treasury.

Premium Bonds

Premium Bonds were launched in 1956 as 'savings products with a thrill'. They encourage people to put money aside with the added incentive that they may win a cash prize. The system for allocating prizes is known as Ernie (Electronic Random Number Indicator Equipment) which was what was used to generate the first set of winning numbers.

Cash prizes are awarded each month, ranging in value from £25 to £1 million, and your winnings are tax free. Unlike playing the lottery, you can cash in your Premium Bonds and get your money back at any time, so they are well worth a flutter. See www.nsandi.com for further details.

Save the change

Lloyds TSB offers a Save the Change debit card, which rounds up your purchases to the next pound and 'saves the change' for you. For example, if you bought a sandwich for £2.65 it would debit £3 from your account, paying the retailer £2.65 and putting the remaining 35p into your savings account. By the end of the year, you could have accumulated over £100 simply through buying your lunch! If you don't want to change bank cards, save the small change yourself by putting it into spare purse or wallet and emptying it into a piggy bank at the end of the week.

Sweep it away

One of the best ways to start saving is to set up a direct debit so that you divert £50 or £75 a month into a savings account. But if like most people your disposable income fluctuates from month to month, you might be reluctant to commit to such a scheme. After all, there may be some months when you find that you can't afford to stash away £50 while in other months you can put aside a lot more. Abbey, First Direct, HSBC, Co-op and Intelligent Finance all offer sweep accounts, which mean that any surplus cash you have sitting in your current account after your monthly outgoings and expenses is automatically 'swept away' into a savings account, where it earns interest.

Investments

Savings products such as cash ISAs and National Savings Bonds are an excellent way to build up a rainy day fund or short-term nest egg, but over the medium and long term there will be more of an increase in a well-managed stock market fund. However, investing in the stock market carries risks. Unlike savings accounts, your money can go up or down at any time. You should not invest in the stock market if you have credit card or loan debts. Nor should you invest money you cannot afford to tie up for at least five years. And you should *never* put your money into investments you do not understand.

On the other hand, if you are debt free (other than your mortgage) and have sufficient cash savings for a rainy day, you should consider making regular savings into a stock market-based investment fund; over the long term it will produce better returns than a cash-based savings product. One of the best ways to invest in the stock market is through a stocks and shares ISA, so that your money grows tax free. As the term implies, you can put all sorts of stocks and shares into an ISA, but the best option is to buy a pooled fund such as a unit or investment trust.

Unit trusts

Unit trusts are pooled funds that buy and sell shares. A large number of people pool their money into the fund, and a fund manager picks shares to buy and sell into the fund. The fund itself is divided into tiny 'units' – each investor owns several units, giving them a tiny share of the overall portfolio. The benefit of putting your money into a pooled fund such as a unit trust is that you spread the risk over a wide portfolio of shares. Buying and selling individual shares is expensive, and most of us do not have the time, money or expertise to buy and monitor a large portfolio. Unit trusts are valued every day, so you can easily check how well your fund is doing.

At present there are 2,000 unit trusts in the UK, and different funds invest in different geographical and industry sectors. For example, some funds invest in North American or Japanese shares, others specialise in large or small UK companies, and others in emerging markets, such as India or China. Some funds specialise in technology or pharmaceutical shares. Over the past five years US and Japanese funds have hardly grown at all and some have lost money, while many emerging market funds have grown by 100 per cent. However, experts agree that your first stock market investment should be a conservative 'safety first' one that invests in funds in your home country.

Investment trusts

Like unit trusts, investments trusts are also pooled investments that buy and sell shares. The crucial difference is that an investment trust is also a company in itself that buys and sells shares to raise money just like any other company. So an investment trust is really a share that invests in shares.

The price of an investment trust depends on the value of its assets – this is known as the trust's net asset value (NAV) – and demands for its own shares as a company in its own right. When the market price of the trust's shares is *less* than the value of the shares inside it, the trust is said to be trading at a discount. When the price of the share is *higher* than the value of the shares within, it is trading at a premium. Canny investors do well by buying investment trusts when they are trading at a discount, and selling them when the discount narrows.

There are currently 440 investment trusts in the UK. Investment trust charges are lower than those of unit trusts, as investment trust companies do not pay commission to independent financial advisers. Research shows that over the long term (more than ten years) investment trusts tend to outperform unit trusts.

Tracker funds

Like unit trusts, tracker funds are pooled investments. However, instead of being run by a fund manager who picks and chooses stocks, the fund simply 'tracks' the performance of a stock market index such as the FTSE 100. Because you are not paying for the services of a fund manager, tracker funds usually do not have an initial charge, and there is a low annual charge of 0.5 per cent to 1 per cent.

Fund supermarkets

Fund supermarkets such as www.fundsnetwork.com and www. cofunds.co.uk allow you to pick and choose investments to put into your stocks and shares ISA. No single funds supermarket will offer every different unit or investment trust that is available on the market. Most offer between 400 and 500, including the most popular.

The benefit of buying your investments from a fund supermarket is that it is cheaper than buying direct from the investment company. As we said, unit trusts have high initial charges of up to 6 per cent, but if you buy from a fund supermarket the fee can be slashed by a third. Many independent financial advisers have their own fund supermarkets or can purchase investments from them on your behalf. This is a good way of both obtaining financial advice and benefiting from supermarket discounts.

Pensions

Financial experts have been warning for several years that we are sitting on a pensions time bomb as we are all living longer and saving less for our retirement. A survey conducted by Scottish Widows in July 2010 found that one-fifth of working adults in the UK have no pension provision in place, and another two-fifths are saving less because of the economic downturn.

Saving for your retirement is an expensive business, so the sooner you start the better. According to financial adviser Chase de Vere, to retire on an income of £30,000 a year a person in their thirties would need to have amassed a pension pot worth £258,000 by the time they were 40, and continue to save a further £375 a month until the age of 60. If you put off pension planning until you are in your 40s, you would need to start saving at least £1,443 a month to retire on an income of £30,000 a year at the age of 65. If you saved just £375 a year, you would achieve an income of just £7,795 a year at 65.

Tax relief

The Inland Revenue (HMRC) gives you tax relief at your highest rate on pension contributions, so a basic rate taxpayer who puts £80 a month into a pension will have their contribution topped up to £100 by the taxman. A higher rate taxpayer needs to find just £60 a month to see £100 a month going into their pension. However, from April 2011 pension tax relief for those with incomes of £150,000 will be restricted so that it is gradually tapered down to the 20 per cent relief, and the 40 per cent relief is likely to disappear completely when your income reaches £180,000. It is rumoured that tax relief on pensions may be removed entirely one day, especially for higher rate earners, so it's a good idea to take advantage of help from the taxman while you can.

Company pensions

If your employer offers a company pension scheme you should take advantage of it, because the company will usually top up your contributions. For example, if your employer deducts 4 per cent of your salary towards your pension, it may contribute an extra 6 per cent of your salary with its own money. If you pay 6 per cent, it may pay in an extra 9 per cent. There may be restrictions on when you can join your company pension scheme (for example, only after two years' service). Contribution amounts will also vary according to your age and the company's scheme.

There are two types of company pension: final-salary pension schemes and money-purchase schemes. Final-salary schemes are usually paid at the rate of one-sixtieth of your final salary multiplied by the number of years you have worked for your employer. Therefore, if you worked for the same employer continuously for 40 years, you would be guaranteed a pension equivalent to two-thirds of your final salary.

Money-purchase pension schemes provide less security and require you to take more control of your retirement fund. Although you know how much money is going into your pension pot, the value of that fund will depend on how well the fund managers have invested your money and on stock market conditions when you retire.

Final-salary pension schemes are fast becoming a thing of the past as the government strives to move the burden of pension provision from the state to the individual.

Personal pensions

If you are self-employed or work for an employer that does not offer a company pension scheme you may have invested in a personal pension scheme or be thinking of doing so. Personal pension schemes are complex, and do not appear in comparison tables, so if you are thinking about buying one, you should obtain good financial advice from a specialist adviser from the outset and keep the performance of the fund under review. Many personal pension schemes have been criticised for the high charges that often eat up the holder's monthly contributions – charges that mean that their pension fund is worth little more (and sometimes less) than the total amount paid in.

Stakeholder pensions

Stakeholder pensions operate in exactly the same way as personal pensions, but they must meet minimum guidelines in terms of charges and contribution arrangements. Stakeholder pensions are regarded as flexible personal pensions because you can stop and start contributions, or vary the level of your contribution, at any time without incurring any financial penalties. The minimum contribution you can make to a stakeholder pension is £20, so stakeholder pensions are a good option for low-paid workers or for women who think they are likely to stop work to have children.

Personal account pensions

In a bid to alleviate poverty in old age for workers in low- and medium-paid jobs, the government is introducing a new national pensions scheme in 2012, which will be known as NEST (National Employment Savings Trust). All employees between the ages of 22 and the state retirement age will be automatically enrolled in the scheme if their employer does not have a pension scheme of its own in place. You can choose to opt out of the scheme if you prefer to make your own pension provision, but you will have to make an active decision to do so. Employees will see 4 per cent of their salary paid into the account, their employers will be required to pay an extra 3 per cent, and the government will chip in 1 per cent tax relief on top. However, pension experts warn that while the default contribution rate into NESTs is better than no personal pension at all, they will not be enough to build up a large enough pension on which to retire comfortably.

State retirement age

The current state retirement age is 60 for women and 65 for men, but this is set to increase gradually to 65 for both men and women by 2020. After this, the retirement age for both men and women is expected to increase to 68 at some point between 2024 and 2046.

Credit cards

Credit cards can be a boon to money savers when they are used correctly. As long as you pay off your card each month you can enjoy up to 56 days of free credit. Credit cards also give you consumer protection, because under the Consumer Credit Act if you pay for any item over £100 but under £30,000 using a credit card, both the card issuer and the trader have equal liability. This means that if the goods are damaged or the company goes into liquidation you are protected and can reclaim your money. These rights apply to items purchased in the UK or abroad in a shop, online, by telephone or by mail order.

Some cards also include price protection, which means that if you purchase an item at a certain price and it is later discounted, you may be able to reclaim the difference, though a time limit of 60 days usually applies.

Many credit cards offer air miles and freebies when you sign up. However, the best type of credit card by far is the cashback credit card, which pays you each time you make a purchase. If you pay off your card each month this really is money for free, and many providers have enticing introductory offers. At the end of 2010 American Express was offering 5 per cent cashback in the first three months, up to a maximum of £100. Typically, cashback cards pay between 0.5 per cent and 1 per cent cashback after the initial honeymoon period. Price comparison tables will help you search for the best credit cards for your needs.

Make more than the minimum repayment

The average APR on credit cards is 16.9 per cent. If you put every-thing on a typical credit card over the festive season and make only minimum repayments each month, it will take you several years to pay off the debt and you'll pay an awful lot in interest, too. For example, if you have a balance of £1,000 on a card levying 16.9 per cent interest and make the minimum monthly payment of 2 per cent (£20) for 12 months, you will rack up £151.74 in interest and have reduced your balance to £920.60. If you increased your monthly payments to £50, you'd pay nearly £30 less in interest and cut the overall balance by nearly £400. And if you paid £100 a month, you'd be almost debt free after 12 months and have paid just £79.16 in interest.

Transfer to a 0% balance transfer card

Paying interest on credit cards is financial madness, so if you can't clear your balance each month, transfer it to a card offering 0 per cent on balance transfers. If you transferred £1,000 on to a 0 per cent balance transfer card and paid £83.33 a month, you'd clear the debt in 12 months without paying a penny in interest.

Don't use 0% credit cards for purchases

Many credit card providers offer 0 per cent on balance transfers and also new purchases. The catch is that whereas the 0 per cent on balance transfers may last for, say, 15 months, the 0 per cent rate on new purchases is usually for a much shorter period. What this means in plain English is that unless you clear the whole amount of the balance transfer and new purchases within three months, you'll end up paying interest at whatever extortionate rate the credit card provider levies on the whole lot. Never use a 0 per cent balance transfer card for further purchases. These cards are strictly for debt management only, and once you have transferred your balance, cut up the card to avoid temptation.

Don't shuffle your debts

If you're clued up on 0 per cent balance transfers and regularly apply for new 0 per cent balance transfer cards to shuffle your debts, you're what the financial services industry rather uncouthly terms a 'rate tart'. Transferring debts between 0 per cent balance transfer cards can be an effective debt-management strategy, but having too many (ten or more) cards can adversely affect your credit rating. Also, be aware that lenders can change or withdraw the 0 per cent deal at any time, so if you can't clear your balance immediately the interest will pile up and you'll be saddled with debts that may take several years to pay off.

Financial advice

If you want to buy a stock market investment or personal pension or if you need advice on complex tax issues such as inheritance tax planning or capital gains tax, you should seek good independent financial advice. Many banks have their own financial advisers, but they will only sell their own products, which are unlikely to provide the best all-round value.

There are two types of financial advice: fee-based advice, for which you pay the adviser an hourly rate, and commission-based advice, for which the adviser receives a commission from the company for the product they sell. A good place to start looking for an independent financial adviser (IFA) in your area is through the IFA promotion website, www.unbiased.co.uk.

How to get good financial advice

1. Make a shortlist of three or four advisers in your area that specialise in the field you are interested in and arrange a consultation. Even a fee-based financial adviser should give you half an hour to discuss your needs.

2. Ask them about their recent work and expertise in their field.

3. If they are fee based ask about their hourly rate and for an estimate of product charges. If they are commission based, ask how much commission they receive for the products they recommend.

4. Ask about their ongoing services. Will they provide an annual review? This is vital if you are investing in a long-term vehicle such as a personal pension. Many financial advisers are eager to snap up new business but are less good at providing ongoing help.

5. Once you have found a financial adviser, they must undertake a full 'fact find' of your finances (your income, mortgage, existing savings and investments, and so on). They will also ask you about your financial objectives – are you saving for university fees, early retirement, a deposit on a home? They will also ask you about your attitude to financial risk.

Quick Reference 2
Debt management

Having debts hanging over your head is stressful and can have a detrimental effect on other areas of your life. One of the most common reactions is to bury your head in the sand by refusing to open bills and letters from creditors and ignoring their phone calls. However, mortgage companies, utility suppliers, banks and credit card companies have long, well-established strategies for recovering debts, and choosing to ignore the problem will result in legal action sooner or later. The sooner you take control of the situation the better.

The six-point plan for getting your finances back on track

1. *Tot up your outgoings.* Make an inventory of all your outgoings, including your mortgage, bills, credit cards and loans. If your total repayments are more than 30 per cent of your net monthly income, you are in danger of slipping into debt. If they add up to 80 per cent of your monthly income or more, you are spending more than you bring in and should follow the next steps to reduce your outgoings.

2. *Prioritise.* If you owe tax, pay this first – in extreme cases, the Inland Revenue can make you bankrupt in a day. Your second priority is to keep a roof over your head, so if you are struggling to pay your mortgage or have arrears on your account, talk to your lender. They may allow you to take a payment holiday for a couple of months while you sort out your finances, or you may be able to reduce your monthly payments by switching to an

interest-only mortgage or extending your mortgage term. Most lenders will not threaten you with repossession if you have a payment plan in place. If you *are* threatened with litigation, take advice from your local Citizens Advice Bureau or Shelter. As well as your mortgage, you should also always pay your council tax, utility bills and TV license to avoid being disconnected and don't forget that you need to make sure you have enough money for food, toiletries and other daily essentials.

3. *Negotiate with creditors on non-priority debts.* Credit cards, loans and overdrafts are regarded as non-priority debts and should be paid after your mortgage, utilities and living expenses. The first step is to write to your creditors, asking them to freeze or reduce the interest you are paying on your debts and to agree a repayment plan. Do not be bullied into paying more than you can afford. If you are currently unemployed, the most you may be able to pay is £1 a month, but this is better than nothing.

4. *Claim your benefits.* If you have lost your job, are on a very low income or have dependents you may be entitled to state benefits.

5. *Get advice.* It is a criminal offence for creditors to harass you for payment. If you feel that you are being harassed or cannot deal with your debts alone, take advice from your local Citizens Advice Bureau or the Consumer Credit Counselling Service. These organisations will help you draw up a budget, and they may negotiate with creditors on your behalf.

6. *Stick to your budget and do not borrow more.* Finally, stick to your budget and repayment agreements and *under no circumstances take on more debt*. Get into the habit of paying for things with cash.

Quick Reference 3
Your money growth calculator

Keeping a record of how much money you are saving each month will give you the incentive to incorporate even more money-saving habits into your daily lifestyle. Record your savings using the table below to see how they add up, and how they are putting you on track to achieving your financial goals. Add in any other money-saving methods you end up using throughout the year.

	£ saving
January Food shopping Selling clutter on eBay	
February Food shopping Lent savings Online surveys	
March Food shopping Clothes shopping	

£ saving

April
Tax savings
Growing your own fruit & veg

May
Holiday savings

June
Food shopping
Picking your own fruit

July
Food shopping
Car boot sales
Selling your own produce

August
Motoring costs
Childcare costs
Back-to-school savings

	£ saving

September
Food shopping
Making extra cash
Switching suppliers

October
Food shopping
Energy savings

November
Food shopping
Homemade presents

December
Christmas food & drink
Decorations

Perfect Answers to Interview Questions

Max Eggert

All you need to get it right first time

- Are you determined to succeed in your job search?
- Do you want to make sure you stand out from the competition?
- Do you want to find out what interviewers *really* want to hear?

Perfect Answers to Interview Questions is essential reading for anyone who's applying for jobs. Written by a leading HR professional with years of experience in the field, it explains the sorts of questions most frequently asked, gives practical advice about how to show yourself in your best light, and provides real-life examples to help you practise at home. Whether you're a graduate looking to take the first step on the career ladder, or you're planning an all-important job change, *Perfect Answers to Interview Questions* will give you the edge.

BOOKS

Perfect CV

Max Eggert

All you need to get it right first time

- Are you determined to succeed in your job search?
- Do you need guidance on how to make a great first impression?
- Do you want to make sure your CV stands out?

Bestselling *Perfect CV* is essential reading for anyone who's applying for jobs. Written by a leading HR professional with years of experience, it explains what recruiters are looking for, gives practical advice about how to show yourself in your best light, and provides real-life examples to help you improve your CV. Whether you're a graduate looking to take the first step on the career ladder, or you're planning an all-important job change, *Perfect CV* will help you stand out from the competition.

BOOKS

Perfect Letters and Emails for All Occasions

George Davidson

All you need to get it right first time

- Do you sometimes find it difficult to get your message across in emails?
- Are you worried that your formal letters are letting you down?
- Do you want some straightforward advice on improving your writing skills?

Perfect Letters and Emails for All Occasions is an invaluable guide for anyone who wants to get the most out of their written communication. Covering everything from advice on how to write to your MP to tips about 'netiquette' and avoiding offensive blunders, it is a one-stop-shop for anyone who wants their writing to get results. Whether you're sending a reply to a formal invitation or a covering letter for a job application, *Perfect Letters and Emails for All Occasions* has all you need to make sure you get your message across elegantly and effectively.

BOOKS

Perfect Presentations

Andrew Leigh and Michael Maynard

All you need to get it right first time

- Have you been asked to give a presentation?
- Would you like some guidance on the best way to deliver your material?
- Do you want to make sure you get your message across effectively?

Perfect Presentations is an invaluable guide for anyone preparing to speak in public. Written by two professional trainers with years of experience in the field, it explains how to plan and structure talks, offers tips on conquering nerves, and gives suggestions for the most effective and inspiring way to deliver your material. Whether you're taking your first steps on the career ladder and want some pointers, or you're a seasoned professional looking to refine your presenting technique, *Perfect Presentations* has all you need to make sure you come across brilliantly.

BOOKS

Perfect Punctuation

Stephen Curtis

All you need to get it right first time

- Do you find punctuation a bit confusing?
- Are you worried that your written English might show you up?
- Do you want a simple way to brush up your skills?

Perfect Punctuation is an invaluable guide to mastering punctuation marks and improving your writing. Covering everything from semi-colons to inverted commas, it gives step-by-step guidance on how to use each mark and how to avoid common mistakes. With helpful examples of correct and incorrect usage and exercises that enable you to practise what you've learned, *Perfect Punctuation* has everything you need to ensure that you never make a mistake again.

BOOKS

Perfect Slow Cooking

Elizabeth Brown

All you need to get it right first time

- Would you like to get the most out of your slow cooker?
- Do you want to create healthy home-cooked meals with the minimum of effort?
- Do you want to save money and time without compromising on taste?

Perfect Slow Cooking is an indispensable guide to this healthy and economical way of preparing meals. Covering everything from how to choose the right appliance to advice on the most affordable cuts of meat, it walks you through every aspect of the slow-cooking method and offers tried-and-tested tips that will help ensure all your meals taste fantastic. With a selection of mouth-watering recipes for soups, curries, roasts and desserts, alternative options for those occasions when you don't have all the ingredients, and useful advice on finding the time to cook during a busy day, *Perfect Slow Cooking* has all you need to prepare delicious, healthy home-cooked meals on a budget.

BOOKS

Perfect Speeches for All Occasions

Matt Shinn

All you need to get it right first time

- Have you been asked to give a speech?
- Are you worried your nerves will get the better of you?
- Do you need some tips on how to deliver your message clearly
  and effectively?

Perfect Speeches for All Occasions is an indispensable guide for
anyone who has to give a talk or presentation. Written by Matt
Shinn, a professional speech writer with years of experience in the
field, it explains how to structure your speech so that it has the most
impact and gives practical advice about controlling your nerves on
the big day. Whether you're been asked to 'say a few words' at a
party or need to put together a high-level presentation, *Perfect
Speeches for All Occasions* has all you need to make sure you perform
with style and confidence.

rh

BOOKS

**Order more titles in the *Perfect* series
from your local bookshop, or have them delivered
direct to your door by Bookpost.**

☐ Perfect Answers to Interview Questions	Max Eggert	9781905211722	£7.99
☐ Perfect CV	Max Eggert	9781905211739	£7.99
☐ Perfect Letters and Emails for All Occasions	George Davidson	9781847945495	£6.99
☐ Perfect Numerical and Logical Test Results	Joanna and Marianna Moutafi	9781847945464	£6.99
☐ Perfect Presentations	Andrew Leigh and Michael Maynard	9781847945518	£6.99
☐ Perfect Punctuation	Stephen Curtis	9781905211685	£6.99
☐ Perfect Slow Cooking	Elizabeth Brown	9781847946058	£6.99
☐ Perfect Speeches for All Occasions	Matt Shinn	9781847945556	£6.99

Free post and packing
Overseas customers allow £2 per paperback

Phone: 01624 677237

Post: Random House Books
c/o Bookpost, PO Box 29, Douglas, Isle of Man IM99 1BQ

Fax: 01624 670 923

email: bookshop@enterprise.net

Cheques (payable to Bookpost) and credit cards accepted

Prices and availability subject to change without notice.
Allow 28 days for delivery.
When placing your order, please state if you do not
wish to receive any additional information.

www.rbooks.co.uk

BOOKS